TEXAS COUNTRY REPORTER COOKBOOK

TEXAS COUNTRY REPORTER

COOKBOOK

RECIPES FROM
THE VIEWERS OF
"TEXAS COUNTRY
REPORTER"

SHEARER PUBLISHING · FREDERICKSBURG, TEXAS

Published in 1990 by
Shearer Publishing
PO BOX 2915
Fredericksburg, Texas 78624

Library of Congress Cataloging in Publication Data
Texas Country Reporter Cookbook
90-092031
ISBN 0-940672-54-5 (PBK)

Designed by Barbara Jezek
Edited by Alison Tartt

Printed in China
Third Edition
Cover design by Barbara Jezek
Back cover photography by Brian Hawkins
10 9 8 7

CONTENTS

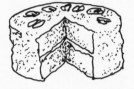

INTRODUCTION

Back in the early 1970s a group of Dallas television producers had a unique idea. "The big cities get plenty of coverage on the nightly news," they said. "Why not hit the backroads and see what the people have to say? We just might be surprised at what we find." And with that, "Texas Country Reporter" was born.

In the early days, the show featured mostly on-the-street interviews about the serious questions of the day. Vietnam. Watergate. But occasional questions like "Does a cow stand up with its front or back legs first?" seemed more popular than war and political corruption, and stories about small towns and general stores became the weekly fare of the show.

Over the years the crew and I have spent a lot of time on Texas backroads, those two-lane blacktop conduits that lead from one small town to the next. We noticed lots of important things during all that driving around, and we became experts on why towns in certain areas seemed to be spaced about the same distance apart (it used to be a day's ride on horseback) and the right person to ask if you're looking for information in a small town (the old guy whittling in front of the courthouse or the kid working the drive-up at the Dairy Queen). And we've learned about Texas food. We've tasted hot links in Pittsburg, kolaches in West, chili in Terlingua, and crawfish in Mauriceville. We found the "best" barbecue in a dozen or more places and the "best" chicken-fried steak in more than that. We learned that hamburgers should be all beef and not laced with pork or tofu. We don't much care for cattail crepes but have learned to appreciate people who do. I, personally, have tasted the best food and the worst food in Texas; and it must have been mostly the best, because I've gained twenty pounds since I started traveling the backroads. My expanding waistline must have tipped off the viewers because for years folks have sent me their favorite recipes. Somehow they knew I like to eat.

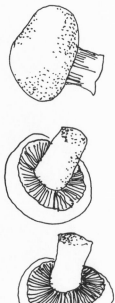

Armed with my collection of recipes from all over Texas and nudged by viewers, another idea was born. "Why not collect more recipes and put 'em in a cookbook?" We asked our viewers to send in their best recipes and received thousands in just a few short weeks. In choosing the recipes for the book, we took into account duplication (we never knew there were so many versions of chicken and dumplings), originality (who would have thought you could serve tumbleweeds as a side dish?), location (from all parts of the state), and, of course, quality. The competition was fierce and the choices were tough. While we did try as many as we could, not every recipe has passed the Bob Phillips taste test. Some recipes just smelled good on paper, and we knew we could count on our friends and viewers being good cooks. Most of the recipes came from our viewers, but some we collected from folks you've seen on the show. I've even put in my own chili recipe, and my wife Tracy has a killer stew in the book.

Two decades ago, we had a unique idea. We thought we'd go out and see what the people had to say. We figured we'd be surprised at what we found. And we were. We're still traveling the Texas backroads, and we're still meeting lots of great folks and having just as much fun as we did twenty years ago. We're glad to share some of what we've found and hope you get as much enjoyment out of it as we have. See ya on the backroads!

Bob Phillips
Dallas

APPETIZERS

Texas Crabgrass

½ cup butter
½ medium onion, diced
1 package frozen spinach, cooked and drained
1 7-ounce can crabmeat, drained
¾ cup Parmesan cheese
melba toast rounds

Melt butter, sauté onions, and add spinach, crabmeat, and cheese. Serve from a chafing dish with melba toast rounds.

Charla Edwards
Panhandle

Great-Great-Grandmaw Korth's Homemade Cheese

1 quart cottage cheese, drained
3 tablespoons margarine
2 tablespoons cream or evaporated milk
3 teaspoons baking soda
2 teaspoons sugar
½ teaspoon salt
caraway seeds to taste (optional)

Mix together cottage cheese, salt, sugar, baking soda, and cream in a glass bowl. Cover bowl with a towel and let stand at room temperature for 5 or 6 hours, stirring occasionally. Blend in margarine and cook over low to medium heat until margarine is melted and well blended. Add caraway seeds and pour into a bowl to cool. Serve on warm sausage bread or homemade bread.

Greg Haston
Angleton

This was my great-great-grandmother's recipe. My mother says that one of her earliest memories was of going to stay with her grandmother and helping to make this cheese. They would spend Saturday mornings making homemade bread for the week to come and this cheese to go on it. It is especially tasty if you make it using homemade cottage cheese curd.

Sombrero Dip

1 15-ounce can ranch-style beans, drained
½ pound lean hamburger meat
1 small onion, chopped
½ cup shredded cheddar cheese
½ cup sliced black olives
½ cup Pace chunky hot salsa

Mix meat and onion together and cook until meat is no longer pink. Drain. Add remaining ingredients and heat until mixture is bubbly and cheese is melted. Serve hot with corn chips. To serve as a main dish, use the beans undrained and add a little water. Serve with hot cornbread.

Edithe Burns
Glen Rose

Fiesta Pecans

1 egg white
¼ cup vegetable oil
¼ teaspoon cayenne pepper
1 tablespoon Worcestershire sauce
½ teaspoon Tabasco sauce
¼ teaspoon black pepper
½ teaspoon salt
2 cups pecan halves
1 teaspoon paprika

Combine first seven ingredients in a bowl; beat well. Add pecans and stir well. Add paprika and toss until pecans are evenly coated. Drain and spread pecan mixture in a single layer in a greased 15″ × 10″ × 1″ jelly-roll pan. Bake at 300 degrees for 25 to 30 minutes, stirring every 10 minutes. Remove to waxed paper while still hot; cool completely. Store in an airtight container in refrigerator up to two weeks. Makes 2 cups.

Ruth Dyer
San Antonio

Hot Crab Dip

1 8-ounce package cream cheese
3 tablespoons mayonnaise
2 tablespoons white wine
1 teaspoon Dijon mustard
½ teaspoon sugar
¼ to ½ teaspoon salt
1 pound crabmeat

In the top of a double boiler, melt cream cheese. Add remaining ingredients and blend until creamy. Add crabmeat and stir carefully.

Genie Cudd
Perryton

My grandmother in Jackson, Mississippi, first began making this recipe, and my mother and I still make it every Thanksgiving and Christmas.

Chicken Feed

1 14- to 16-ounce box Corn Chex cereal
1 14- to 16-ounce box Rice Chex cereal
1 14- to 15-ounce box Cheerios
1 12- to 14-ounce box pretzel sticks
1 or 2 8-ounce cans mixed nuts
6 sticks margarine
½ cup Worcestershire sauce
3 tablespoons Tabasco sauce
2 tablespoons bacon drippings
2 tablespoons garlic salt

Mix cereals, pretzels, and nuts in a large baking pan. Melt butter and mix with Worcestershire sauce, Tabasco sauce, bacon drippings, and garlic salt. Pour over dry mixture. Stir to coat. Bake at 250 degrees for 1 hour, stirring every 15 minutes.

Donna Ingram
Irving

Cold Marinated Shrimp

2 pounds shrimp (35–40 count), shelled and boiled
2 white onions, sliced thin
10 whole bay leaves

MARINADE
1½ cups vegetable oil
½ cup white vinegar
3½ teaspoons celery seed
1 teaspoon salt
3 teaspoons undrained capers
1 teaspoon Tabasco sauce

Combine marinade ingredients and mix well. Layer shrimp in deep bowl. Cover with layer of onions and some bay leaves and repeat layers until shrimp is used up. Pour marinade over shrimp and refrigerate 24 hours. Stir occasionally.

Gregor C. MacGregor
Dallas

Cheese Ball

2 8-ounce packages cream cheese, softened
10 ounces grated cheddar cheese
1 package Hidden Valley Ranch Mix Original Flavor
chopped pecans (optional)

Mix all ingredients except pecans and roll into two balls or logs. Then roll in chopped pecans and serve with an assortment of crackers.

Angela Graves
Buffalo

Empanadas, Panama Style

MEAT FILLING
2 pounds ground beef
1 large onion, chopped
5 or 6 jalapeño peppers, chopped
½ teaspoon garlic powder
4 teaspoons sweet basil
¾ teaspoon salt
1 8-ounce package cream cheese

DOUGH
2 sticks margarine
1 8-ounce package cream cheese
½ teaspoon salt
6 cups flour

To make filling, combine all ingredients except cream cheese in a skillet. Brown until meat is done. Add small cubes of cream cheese, stirring until cheese is melted. Remove from heat. To make dough, mix all ingredients in order listed. Divide into small golf-ball-size portions. Roll each ball out flat to form circle. Fill circles with meat filling. Fold over and seal edges by pressing with the tines of a fork. Bake at 350 degrees for 15 to 20 minutes until brown. Serve hot with or without catsup on the side. Makes 30 to 32.

Gen Mullins
Fort Worth

These meat pies are great for buffets, club meetings, and snacks. Three or four can make a meal. I got the recipe from a Panamanian cook who was working in the Tripoli Hotel while we were stationed in the Canal Zone with the Air Force.

Tapas

1½ pounds cheddar cheese, grated
½ pound jalapeño cheese, grated
2 cups ham, chopped
1 cup flour
2 eggs
1 large can evaporated milk

Mix the cheeses and ham and press into a greased 9″ × 12″ pan. Mix flour, eggs, and milk and pour over ham and cheese mixture. Bake at 350 degrees 35 to 40 minutes or until brown. Cut into bite-size pieces. Spear each piece with a toothpick and serve.

Carolyn Coleman
Dallas

Cream Cheese Pinwheel

2 8-ounce packages cream cheese
3 fresh jalapeños, chopped fine
4 green onions, chopped fine
24 flour tortillas at room temperature

Mix cream cheese until soft and creamy, then add green onions and jalapeños. Mix in cheese. Add a drop or two of milk if needed to thin the spread. Spread mixture on each tortilla and roll tortilla. Chill overnight. When ready to serve, cut into ½-inch-wide slices and serve.

Kay Hall
Brady

Armadillo Eggs

1 pound Monterey Jack cheese, grated and divided
½ pound hot pork sausage
1½ cups buttermilk biscuit mix
1 package Shake 'n Bake mix for pork
15 small to medium canned jalapeño peppers
2 eggs, beaten

Slit and seed peppers. Stuff peppers with half the cheese and pinch peppers closed around the cheese. Mix remaining cheese and sausage. Add dry biscuit mix, one-third at a time, to make a stiff dough. Knead several times. Pinch off a bit of dough and pat into a flat pancake about ½ inch thick. Place a stuffed pepper in the middle of each pancake and wrap completely with dough, making sure that all edges and ends are sealed. Roll the dough-covered pepper in your hands to mold into an egg shape. Roll in Shake 'n Bake until coated. Dip in beaten eggs and roll again in Shake 'n Bake. Bake at 300 degrees for 20 to 25 minutes.

Vanita Hull
Mansfield

Shrimp Dip

1 8-ounce package cream cheese, softened
1 cup mayonnaise (not salad dressing)
¼ cup milk
⅓ cup onion flakes
1 teaspoon dill
1 teaspoon Accent
½ teaspoon Tabasco sauce (optional)
3 stalks celery, chopped fine
1 4- to 6-ounce can small deveined shrimp

Combine all ingredients except shrimp and mix until smooth. Crumble shrimp into mixture and stir until blended. Refrigerate overnight. Serve with Ritz crackers.

Marsha Watkins
Pearland

Chiles Rellenos

1½ cups cheddar cheese, grated
1½ cups Monterey Jack cheese, grated
2 4-ounce cans whole green chilies
2 5-ounce cans evaporated milk
3 eggs

Mix the two cheeses together in a bowl. In a round cake dish or square baking dish place one-half of the cheese mixture on the bottom. Lay green chilies flat on top of the cheese. Place remaining cheese mixture on top. In a bowl, mix together eggs and evaporated milk. Pour evenly over mixture. Bake at 325 degrees for about 25 minutes. Top with guacamole, sour cream, or salsa.

Karen Foster-Ryan
Mansfield

Tamale Balls

1 pound ground beef
1 pound ground pork
salt and pepper to taste
1¾ cups masa harina
¾ cup tomato juice
3 cloves garlic, crushed
1 teaspoon cumin

SAUCE
3 16-ounce cans tomatoes
1 tablespoon chili powder
2 teaspoons salt
1 clove garlic, minced

Mix meats. Add salt and pepper to taste. Then add masa harina, tomato juice, garlic, and cumin. Shape into small balls about the size of a walnut. To make sauce, heat all ingredients in a large flat roaster. Bring to a boil. Drop balls into sauce and simmer about 2 hours. (After 1 hour, this can be transferred to a slow cooker until ready to serve.) This recipe freezes well.

Lois Wolff
Kenedy

This extra-special dip was a big hit when our Uncle Herschel Baker from Nacogdoches brought it to a family reunion a couple of years ago.

Uncle Herschel's Fruit Dip

1 8-ounce package cream cheese, softened
1 small jar marshmallow cream
cinnamon to taste

Mix all ingredients until well blended. Serve with strawberries, pineapple, peaches, tangerines, or any other fruit you like.

Dale and Donna Baker
Kilgore

SOUPS

The Puddin Hill Store's Luncheon Experience (as we call our deli/restaurant) features a homemade soup every day. The soup of the day has built up such a loyal following that we publish the menu a month in advance and have regulars who show up whenever their favorite soup is on the menu. The regulars always show up for this one.

East Texas Red Bean Gumbo

2 15-ounce cans pinto beans, undrained
1 10-ounce can Ro-tel tomatoes, undrained
6 tablespoons vegetable oil
6 tablespoons flour
2 medium onions, chopped fine
1 bell pepper, seeded and chopped fine
1 pound cooked smoked sausage, cut into ½-inch slices
1½ cups water
½ cup grated hot pepper cheese

Puree beans and their liquid in a blender or food processor; set aside. Repeat with tomatoes. In a large pot, heat oil and slowly add flour, using a wire whisk to blend. When well blended, stir constantly with a wooden spoon until mixture has turned a light brown color. Add onions and cook, stirring constantly, until translucent. Add bell pepper and sliced sausage, stirring about 5 minutes or until sausage is browned and pepper is softened. Add pureed beans, tomatoes, and water; bring to a boil. Reduce heat and simmer 30 to 40 minutes. Garnish each serving with 1 tablespoon grated pepper cheese. Serves 8.

Mary Lauderdale
Greenville

Campout Soup

1 pound ground beef
½ cup chopped bell pepper
½ cup chopped onion
2 tablespoons chili powder
2 cans chili beef soup, undiluted
½ cup water
1 16-ounce can tomatoes, cut up
1 15½-ounce can kidney beans, undrained

In large saucepan, brown beef, bell pepper, and onion with chili powder. Drain off grease. Stir to separate meat. Add remaining ingredients. Simmer 15 minutes, stirring often. Makes about 8 cups.

Joan Hallford
Fort Worth

Bob's Tortilla Soup

2 cloves garlic, chopped
1 cup chopped yellow or white onions
1 4-ounce can diced green chilies
1 to 2 tablespoons corn oil
8 cups chicken stock (or 2 cans chicken broth, thinned to taste
   with water)
1 teaspoon ground cumin (or to taste)
1 teaspoon white pepper
¼ to ½ teaspoon salt
4 corn tortillas, cut into julienne strips (½ to ¾ inch wide)
corn or peanut oil for frying

In a 3-quart saucepan sauté garlic, onion, and green chilies in hot corn oil for 5 to 10 minutes or until onions are golden in color. Stir in chicken stock and simmer uncovered for 30 to 45 minutes. Add seasonings. A small amount of cornmeal can be added if a thicker soup is desired. Meanwhile, heat 3 to 4 inches corn or peanut oil to 375 to 400 degrees. Fry tortilla strips a few at a time until crisp. Drain on paper towels, sprinkle with salt if desired, and set aside. When ready to serve, reheat soup if needed. Place fried tortilla strips into serving bowls and ladle soup on top. Serve with the following garnishes: diced avocado, shredded or slivered chicken breast, grated or shredded cheeses (asadero, Monterey Jack, cheddar, mozzarella, or any combination of these), cilantro, sour cream.

Robert Helton
El Paso

Okra Gumbo

1 pound extra-lean hamburger meat
1 pound frozen okra
1 16-ounce can stewed tomatoes
1 8-ounce can tomato sauce
1 large onion, sliced
picante sauce to taste

Sauté meat and drain on paper towel. Combine all ingredients in large stewpot. Cook until okra turns color.

Vanora Morris
San Antonio

This recipe is simple and easy to make. I have had many people tell me they don't like okra but they really enjoy my gumbo.

Black Bean Soup

2 cups black beans
8 cups water
1 large onion, chopped
2 or 3 bay leaves
1 clove garlic
2 tablespoons parsley
1 or 2 ham hocks
salt to taste
4 slices bacon
1 bell pepper, chopped
1 teaspoon cumin
2 stalks celery, chopped

Wash beans and cover with water. Bring to a boil and boil for 5 minutes. Turn off heat and let stand for 1 hour. Sauté bacon, onion, bell pepper, and celery. Add to beans with remaining ingredients. Bring to a boil, then lower heat. Simmer until beans are done. Remove bay leaves and ham hocks. Puree about half of beans to thicken soup. Dice ham hock and return to soup. Then serve.

Fred, Penny, and Ady Stiles
Fort Worth

Broccoli Soup

1 10-ounce package frozen chopped broccoli
2 potatoes, peeled and cubed
⅓ cup uncooked rice
1 cup chopped onion
1 tablespoon margarine
5 cups water
2 cans cream of mushroom soup
1 can Ro-tel tomatoes, diced
1 cup Velveeta or other cheese (or 1 can cheddar cheese soup)
salt and pepper to taste

Mix first six ingredients, bring to a boil, and boil 25 to 30 minutes. Add remaining ingredients. Heat mixture but do not boil.

Hellen Kramp
Garland

Dolores's Broccoli-Squash Soup

1 pound extra-lean ground beef
2 cans tomato sauce
1 can tomato paste
2 cups water
1 large bunch broccoli, chopped
4 medium yellow squash, sliced
1 teaspoon sugar
salt and pepper to taste

Brown meat in large pot. Drain off excess fat. Add tomato sauce, tomato paste, water, and sugar. Mix well, cover, and cook slowly for about 20 minutes. Add broccoli, squash, sugar, and salt and pepper. Continue cooking until vegetables are tender but not overcooked.

Dolores R. Booher
Irving

Broccoli-Cheese Soup

1½ cups broccoli
½ cup chopped onion
1 bay leaf
1½ cups milk
2½ tablespoons flour
1½ cups chicken broth
½ teaspoon salt
¼ teaspoon pepper
½ teaspoon Worcestershire sauce
1½ cups grated cheddar cheese, divided

Wash and then steam broccoli approximately 8 minutes. Sauté onion and bay leaf until onion is clear. Discard bay leaf. Heat milk and thicken with flour. Add chicken broth and seasonings. Add broccoli and onion, then half the grated cheese. Cook 3 to 5 minutes. Transfer to individual ramekins or oven casserole. Top with remaining cheese. Heat in medium oven just until cheese melts. Serves 4.

Connie Payne
Keller

Thick Vegetable Soup

ground beef or turkey (any amount desired)
1 No. 2½ can tomatoes
½ cup diced celery
1½ cups diced carrots
1 cup chopped onions
2 cups diced potatoes
½ cup uncooked rice, washed
3½ teaspoons salt
3 cups water

Brown meat lightly, then add remaining ingredients. Simmer 45 minutes.

Mrs. R. W. Burns
Keller

My grandmother, Carrie Morgan, was the cook on the JA Ranch in the Texas Panhandle from 1948 to 1955. She cooked at the mess hall at ranch headquarters, and my grandfather did odd jobs and helped with the cooking and dishwashing. Grannie Morgan made a pot of this soup every day, using plenty of pepper, and served it as the appetizer for the noon meal, which was the main meal of the day.

Grannie Morgan's Vegetable Beef Soup

2 quarts water
1 large meaty beef knuckle bone
1 medium onion, chopped
4 medium potatoes, peeled and chopped
2 stalks celery, diced
1 large can tomatoes, chopped
1 can whole-kernel corn
1 can sweet peas
1 can carrots
1 teaspoon sugar
salt and pepper to taste

Boil knuckle bone in water until meat is tender enough to fall from bone. Remove bone and gristle. To meat and broth add onion, potatoes, celery, and tomatoes. Boil until potatoes and onions are tender. Add remaining vegetables and seasonings. Boil until completely heated through.

Carolyn Jackson
Carrollton

Vegetarian Stew

2 to 3 cups defatted chicken stock or vegetable stock
4 medium potatoes, peeled and cubed
4 carrots, scraped and chopped
3 turnips, peeled and cubed
3 to 4 tomatoes, chopped
6 stalks celery, sliced
4 onions, chopped
5 cloves garlic, minced or crushed
1 7-ounce can chopped green chilies, undrained
2 tablespoons reduced-sodium soy sauce
2 tablespoons basil
¼ cup cornstarch
¼ cup cold water
2 cups frozen green peas

Bring stock to a boil. Add all remaining ingredients except cornstarch, water, and green peas. Simmer, covered, about 25 minutes or until tender. Stir cold water into cornstarch and mix until smooth. Add paste slowly to stew, stirring constantly as stew thickens. Add peas and simmer a few more minutes or until they are heated through. Serve with hot cornbread and tossed salad.

Nawona Bullard
Odessa

This vegetarian stew is so delicious you won't miss the meat.

Gazpacho Italiano

6 medium ripe tomatoes, peeled and quartered
3 small zucchini squash, unpeeled and cut into chunks
1 medium cucumber, peeled and cut into chunks
1 medium green bell pepper, seeded and cut into chunks
1 medium Bermuda onion, peeled and cut into chunks
6 or 7 cloves garlic, peeled and minced
⅓ cup olive oil
juice from 3 lemons (or ¼ cup wine vinegar)
1 teaspoon lemon pepper
6 to 10 drops Tabasco or other hot pepper sauce
1 teaspoon Italian seasoning or oregano
2 tablespoons Worcestershire sauce

Blend all ingredients in blender or food processor. Chill thoroughly in refrigerator. Serve in thoroughly chilled cups or bowls, garnished with croutons.

Alan Thistle
San Antonio

This family favorite has been tried and tested many times. This is not fancy, gourmet cooking; this is down-home good food!

Sausage-Vegetable Soup

4 tablespoons wild rice
3 tablespoons long-grain white rice
2 14½-ounce cans beef broth
8 cups water
2 medium carrots, diced
2 stalks celery, diced
½ medium onion, chopped
1 10-ounce package frozen black-eyed peas
1 14½-ounce can stewed tomatoes, chopped but not drained
1 tablespoon Worcestershire sauce
¼ teaspoon minced garlic
¼ teaspoon oregano leaves
¼ teaspoon thyme leaves
½ teaspoon chili powder
1 teaspoon lemon juice
2 medium potatoes, cubed
1¼ pounds Polish kielbasa, sliced and cut into half or quarter
  circles

Cook both kinds of rice in broth and water for 30 minutes. Add carrots, celery, onion, tomatoes, black-eyed peas, Worcestershire sauce, seasonings, and lemon juice and cook another 30 minutes. Add potatoes and sausage, and cook 10 to 15 minutes more or until potatoes are done.

Fara Murray
Carrollton

Cheese Soup

½ cup fine-chopped carrots
½ cup fine-chopped onions
¼ cup fine-chopped celery
2 tablespoons butter
¼ cup flour
dash of salt
1 cup chicken broth
2 cups light cream or milk
1½ cups shredded American cheese

Cook carrots, onions, and celery in butter. Stir in flour; add salt and broth. Cook and stir until bubbly. Stir in cream or milk, and add cheese; cook until cheese is melted. Do not allow soup to boil. You can also add broccoli or cauliflower if you wish.

Barbara English
Hawley

Knife and Fork Soup

1½ pounds smoked sausage links, cut into pieces (or
  frankfurters)
1 cup thin-sliced carrots
1 cup sliced celery
1 1½-ounce package dry onion soup mix
2 tablespoons sugar
1 teaspoon salt
6 cups boiling water
1 28-ounce can tomatoes
1 5½-ounce package dehydrated hash browns with onions
1 10-ounce package frozen sliced okra or green beans
¼ teaspoon oregano
¼ teaspoon hot pepper sauce

In 4- to 6-quart Dutch oven, combine sausage, carrots, celery,
soup mix, sugar, and salt. Add boiling water, stir, and heat to
boiling. Reduce heat and simmer covered for 10 minutes. Mix in
tomatoes, breaking up with a large spoon. Add potatoes, okra,
oregano, and pepper sauce. Heat to boiling. Reduce heat and simmer covered 30 to 40 minutes or until vegetables are tender. Stir
once or twice. Ladle into large bowls. Serve with crusty bread.
Makes 3 quarts.

Betty Rapp
Corpus Christi

Potato-Cheese Soup

½ stick margarine
1 1-pound package carrots, chopped
1 stalk celery, chopped
1 large onion, chopped
3 14½-ounce cans Swanson's chicken broth
3 10-ounce cans cream of potato soup
1 pound Velveeta cheese
1 cup sour cream (optional)

Sauté carrots, celery, and onion in margarine. Add chicken broth.
Simmer 30 minutes or until vegetables are tender. Add potato
soup and cheese. Simmer 10 minutes, stirring often so cheese
doesn't sink to the bottom and stick. Add sour cream just before
serving.

Pauline King
Centerville

Spicy Chicken Soup

1 2½- to 3-pound broiler or fryer
1 tablespoon salt
½ cup butter or margarine
1 quart boiling water
1 large potato, cubed
1 medium onion, chopped coarse
2 17-ounce cans cream-style corn
1 15-ounce can tomatoes, undrained
1 10-ounce can tomatoes with green chilies, undrained
½ teaspoon pepper

Combine chicken, salt, butter, and boiling water. Bring to a boil, reduce heat, and cook until chicken is tender. Remove chicken from broth; let cook and remove meat from bones. Add potatoes and onion to broth. Bring to a boil; reduce heat and cook vegetables until tender. Add chicken and remaining ingredients. Simmer 30 to 45 minutes, stirring occasionally. Serves 8.

Cathy Gray
Lancaster

Country Creole Split-Pea Soup

1 16-ounce package split peas
10 cups water
2 carrots, sliced
2 ribs celery, sliced
½ cup chopped onion
⅛ teaspoon cayenne pepper
¾ teaspoon salt
¾ teaspoon creole seasoning (or substitute 2 tablespoons salt,
    1 tablespoon ground red pepper, 1 tablespoon chili powder,
    1 teaspoon garlic powder, and 1 teaspoon black pepper)
½ teaspoon white pepper
½ teaspoon Tabasco sauce
½ pound ham, chopped

Wash and drain peas. Combine all ingredients in Dutch oven or stewpot and bring to a boil. Cook over medium heat 15 minutes. Reduce heat, cover, and cook over low heat about 1½ hours. Cool and put through food processor or electric blender. Serves 12.

Mrs. Jack Euwer
Cumby

SALADS

T his salad is delicious served with Thanksgiving and Christmas dinners or with almost any kind of meat. It also keeps well.

Cranberry Salad

1 small package lemon Jell-O
1 cup sugar
1 cup boiling water
2 cups cranberries, ground
½ orange, chopped fine
1 cup chopped pecans
1 cup celery, chopped fine
½ apple, chopped fine

Dissolve Jell-O and sugar in boiling water and let cool. Add remaining ingredients and mix. Chill in salad bowl until congealed.

Ima Ray Watson
Leona

Ribbon Salad

2 packages lime Jell-O
1 package lemon Jell-O
2 packages cherry Jell-O
½ cup miniature marshmallows
1 8-ounce package cream cheese
1 20-ounce can crushed pineapple
1 cup mayonnaise
1 cup whipping cream

In a 9″ × 13″ glass casserole dish, mix cherry Jell-O with 2 cups hot water and 2 cups cold water. Chill until firm. In the top of a double boiler, mix lemon Jell-O with 1 cup hot water and drained juice from pineapple. Add marshmallows and heat until melted. Remove from heat and add cream cheese. Beat until smooth. Cool slightly, then add crushed pineapple and mayonnaise. Fold in whipped cream and chill until thick. Pour over cherry Jell-O and sprinkle with chopped nuts. Mix lime Jell-O with 2 cups hot water and 2 cups cold water. Chill until thick and pour over lemon Jell-O layer. Chill for 24 hours. Serves 24.

Betty Norton
Amarillo

Yum Yum Salad

1 15-ounce can crushed pineapple
⅔ cup sugar
1 3-ounce package orange-pineapple or orange Jell-O
1 3-ounce package cream cheese
1 cup chopped peeled apple
1 cup chopped celery
1 cup chopped pecans
1 small container Cool Whip

Combine pineapple and sugar in a saucepan and boil 3 minutes. Remove from heat and stir in Jell-O. Add cream cheese and refrigerate until slightly thick. Add remaining ingredients and mix thoroughly. Pour into a mold and chill. Serves 8 to 10.

Pauline Duren
Dallas

Light Luscious Lime Salad

1 12-ounce can diet Sprite
1 3-ounce package Philadelphia Lite cream cheese
1 small package sugar-free lime Jell-O
1 small can unsweetened crushed pineapple
½ cup chopped pecans

Heat diet Sprite and mix with cream cheese until dissolved. Strain. Mix together sugar-free Jell-O and crushed pineapple. Add Sprite and cheese mixture and pecans. Refrigerate until congealed.

Madelyn Talkington
Pleasanton

I made this many years with regular ingredients. Then I found out I had diabetes, so I started making it with the sugar-free ingredients. It's still great!

Texas Holiday Salad

2 3-ounce packages strawberry-banana Jell-O
2 cups boiling water
1 10-ounce package frozen strawberries
3 or 4 ripe bananas, mashed
1 16-ounce can crushed pineapple
1 8-ounce container sour cream
1 cup fine-chopped pecans

Mix strawberry-banana Jell-O in boiling water and chill until syrupy. Add strawberries, bananas, and pineapple. Pour half of mixture into a straight-sided glass bowl. Refrigerate until firm. When set, cover with a layer of sour cream. Add pecans to reserved half of Jell-O mixture and pour over sour cream layer. Refrigerate to set firmly. Cover with plastic wrap until ready to use.

Travis and Tama Ernesteen Myrick
Kemp

W hen I was a child, the only time we had fresh fruit was on Christmas Day. Santa left each of us children an apple and an orange, and we contributed our fruit to the fruit salad for Christmas dinner. My mother continued that tradition as long as any of us could come home for Christmas. The younger generations in my family continue to carry on this tradition, even though they have fruit year round and do not have to walk long distances to pick up the pecans.

Grandmother's Fresh Fruit Salad

5 apples, cut into bite-size pieces
5 oranges, cut into bite-size pieces
3 stalks celery, diced
2 cups chopped pecans
1 small jar maraschino cherries, drained
1 teaspoon nutmeg
2 teaspoons cinnamon
3 bananas, sliced

Mix apples, oranges, and celery in a very large bowl. Add cherries, nuts, and spices. Mix well. Chill in refrigerator until ready to use. Immediately before serving, add bananas.

Mattie Alexander Mauldin
Lubbock

T his recipe came from an old *Progressive Farmer* magazine years ago. It's sure good.

Orange Jell-O Salad

1 large package orange Jell-O
1 cup hot water
3 cups cold water
2 cups grated carrots
½ cup crushed pineapple, drained
½ cup coconut
½ cup chopped pecans

Dissolve Jell-O in hot water, then add cold water; mix well. Refrigerate until mixture starts to congeal. Add remaining ingredients. Refrigerate until congealed.

Maymee Vaughan
Benbrook

Texas Caviar

1 pound dried black-eyed peas
2 cups Italian dressing
2 cups diced bell pepper
1½ cups diced onion
1 cup chopped green onion
½ cup fine-chopped jalapeño pepper
1 tablespoon fine-chopped garlic
salt and hot pepper sauce to taste
lettuce leaves

Soak peas 6 hours or overnight. Drain and bring to boil in fresh water. Cook 40 minutes. Drain well. In a large bowl blend with dressing and cool. Add remaining ingredients except lettuce. Chill for several hours to blend flavors. Serve on lettuce leaves.

Ellen A. Lloyd
Aransas Pass

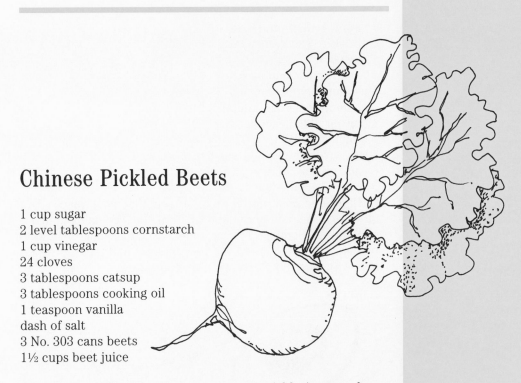

Chinese Pickled Beets

1 cup sugar
2 level tablespoons cornstarch
1 cup vinegar
24 cloves
3 tablespoons catsup
3 tablespoons cooking oil
1 teaspoon vanilla
dash of salt
3 No. 303 cans beets
1½ cups beet juice

Mix sugar and cornstarch in a saucepan. Add vinegar, cloves, catsup, oil, vanilla, and salt and mix well. Cut beets into bite-size pieces. Add beets and beet juice to mixture. Cook over medium heat about 3 minutes or until thick. Store in container in refrigerator.

Joyce Lopanec
New Braunfels

Wilted Lettuce

leaf lettuce
6 slices thick-sliced bacon
4 tablespoons bacon grease
1 tablespoon sugar
2 tablespoons vinegar

Break lettuce into bite-size pieces. In a frying pan, fry bacon until crisp. Remove bacon from pan and crumble into a bowl; add lettuce and mix. To reserved bacon grease, add sugar and vinegar and heat over low heat, stirring until sugar is dissolved. Pour over lettuce, toss, and serve.

Evelyn Frizzell
Killeen

Tex-Mex Salad

1 pound lean ground beef
1 15-ounce can kidney beans, drained
1 teaspoon salt
1 head lettuce, chopped
1 medium onion, chopped
4 medium tomatoes, chopped
1 cup shredded cheddar cheese
1 8-ounce package tortilla chips, crushed (or corn chips)
1 large avocado, peeled, seeded, and sliced
commercial salad dressing (optional)

Cook ground meat until brown, stirring into small pieces. Drain off excess fat. Add beans and salt, stirring well, and simmer for 10 minutes. Combine lettuce, onion, tomatoes, cheese, and tortilla chips in large bowl. Add beef mixture and toss lightly. Garnish with avocado. Serve with salad dressing.

Inez Adams
Paris

Italian Salad

1 12-ounce can Progresso cannellina beans
2 green onions, chopped
½ cup chopped tomatoes
1 small purple onion, chopped
½ cup chopped cucumber
1 cup feta cheese
¼ cup olive oil
⅛ cup vinegar
1 teaspoon garlic salt
1 teaspoon oregano
½ teaspoon pepper
1 teaspoon dill

Mix all ingredients and chill for 1 hour before serving.

Deborah Vinson
Manvel

Pasta Salad

DAY 1
1 16-ounce package vermicelli
1 tablespoon Accent seasoning
1 tablespoon seasoned salt
3 tablespoons lemon juice
4 tablespoons oil

DAY 2
4 ounces pimiento, drained
1 cup bell pepper, diced fine
¾ cup onion, diced fine
1 small can diced black olives, drained
2 cups diced celery
1½ cups mayonnaise

Slightly undercook vermicelli and drain; rinse with cold water
and drain again. Mix remaining ingredients for Day 1 with pasta
and marinate overnight. Combine all ingredients for Day 2 and
add to ingredients mixed on Day 1. Marinate overnight.

Eva Mac McClure
Dallas

End-of-the-Paycheck Pasta Salad

2 cups uncooked shells, elbows, spirals, or spaghetti
½ cup sour cream
1 tablespoon picante sauce

Cook the pasta and drain. Mix sour cream and picante sauce. Add
to pasta, stir well, and serve.

Jerry Wilson
Corpus Christi

Chicken Salad

This dish evolved
from a crisis—a long
day of work and some
very hungry children
wanting to be fed. The
family liked it so much
that it has become an
often-requested favorite
at home and among
friends who have shared
our table with us.

1 package Skinner Garden-Style Twirls
2 to 3 cups diced cooked chicken
1 cup chopped pecans
2 stalks celery, diced
1 small onion, diced
1 small bell pepper, cut into strips
1 carrot, slivered
reduced-calorie ranch-style dressing
seasoned salt to taste
pepper to taste

Cook noodles according to package directions. Drain and cool.
Meanwhile, mix together chicken, pecans, celery, onion, bell pepper, and carrot in a large bowl. Add noodles and toss together.
Add dressing to moisten all ingredients. Add seasoned salt and
pepper. Chill. Serve with crackers or a good French bread. Serves
6 to 8.

Cyndy P. Zachry
Kerrville

Gulf Coast Shrimp Salad

1 tablespoon unflavored gelatin
¼ cup cold water
2 3-ounce packages cream cheese, softened
¼ cup mayonnaise
1 10½-ounce can tomato soup
2 cups shrimp, cleaned, cooked, and cut into bite-size pieces
1 cup diced celery
1 tablespoon fine-chopped bell pepper
1 teaspoon minced onion
½ cup stuffed olives, cut in half

Soak gelatin in cold water. Mix cream cheese and mayonnaise, blending well. Dilute tomato soup with equal amount of water. Heat to boiling, add gelatin, and stir until dissolved. Add slowly to cream cheese mixture. When slightly thickened, add shrimp and vegetables. Pour into an 8-inch square mold and chill until firm. Serve on lettuce or endive. Serves 12.

Maurine Floyd
Corpus Christi

Calico Salad

1 can shoepeg corn
1 can small peas
1 can French-style green beans

DRESSING
½ cup vinegar
½ cup sugar
¼ cup oil
½ teaspoon salt
2 teaspoons pepper (optional)

Drain all vegetables well and mix together. Mix the dressing ingredients in a saucepan and bring to a boil. When cooled, pour over vegetables.

Betty Sullivan
Cold Springs

VEGETABLES

Spence Hearn, noted for his handmade taffy, was the candymaker at the Crystal Palace in Tampa before it closed forty years ago.

Sautéed Asparagus

1 pound fresh asparagus
2 tablespoons butter or margarine
garlic powder or garlic salt to taste
salt and pepper to taste
¼ cup Parmesan cheese

Wash and cut asparagus into 1-inch pieces. Melt butter in skillet over medium-high heat. Lightly sauté asparagus and seasonings about 2 to 3 minutes. Toss with Parmesan cheese and sauté about 1 minute more. Serve.

Mitzi Johnson
Burleson

Asparagus–Water Chestnut Casserole

2 14½-ounce cans cut asparagus
1 can sliced water chestnuts, drained
1 can cream of mushroom soup
buttered bread crumbs

Alternate layers of asparagus and water chestnuts in an oven-proof baking dish. Pour soup over layers. Top with buttered bread crumbs and bake at 350 degrees 20 to 25 minutes.

Mrs. Spence Hearn
Pampa

Broccoli Elegant

1 8- to 10-ounce package cornbread stuffing mix
2 10-ounce packages frozen broccoli spears, thawed and cut into large pieces
¼ cup butter or margarine
¼ cup flour
2 teaspoons chicken-flavored bouillon granules
1½ cups milk
1 8-ounce package cream cheese, softened
½ teaspoon salt
5 to 6 green onions, sliced
1 cup grated cheddar cheese

Prepare cornbread stuffing mix according to package directions. Spoon stuffing around inside edge of a lightly greased 13″ × 9″ baking pan, leaving a well in the center. Place thawed broccoli in center of baking pan and set aside. In a medium saucepan, melt butter over low heat and add flour, stirring until smooth. Cook 1 minute, stirring constantly. Stir in bouillon, then gradually add milk and cook over medium heat, stirring constantly until thickened and bubbly. Break cream cheese into small pieces and add to mixture with salt, stirring until smooth. Stir in onions. Pour mixture mostly over broccoli in center, with a little on the cornbread mixture. Sprinkle with grated cheese. Cover with aluminum foil and bake at 350 degrees for 35 minutes. Remove foil and bake an additional 10 minutes.

Fara Murray
Carrollton

Broccoli and Rice Casserole

1 10-ounce package frozen broccoli
¾ cup uncooked rice
1 onion, chopped
1 stick margarine
1 small jar Cheese Whiz
1 can cream of mushroom soup

Cook broccoli; drain and chop. Cook rice. Sauté onion in the margarine. Combine all ingredients and place in a 2-quart casserole dish. Bake at 350 degrees for 30 minutes. Serves 15.

Nell and Eddie Johnson
Hearne

Eddie Johnson, is a retired railroad man who makes wooden model trains. His second locomotive contained over 6,000 individual parts.

Delicious Cabbage

1 medium onion, chopped
2 tablespoons bacon drippings or shortening
1 small head of cabbage, sliced
1 bell pepper, sliced
2 fresh tomatoes, sliced
salt and pepper to taste

Brown onion in bacon drippings or shortening; remove onions from pan. Place one-third of the sliced cabbage in pan, followed by half of the bell pepper, one tomato, and half the browned onion. Layer with another one-third of the cabbage and remaining bell pepper, tomato, and onions. Sprinkle remaining cabbage on top and add salt and pepper. Cover and cook about 20 minutes or until done.

Linda Coker
Lubbock

Cauliflower Cheese Puff

1 large cauliflower
1½ cups medium-thick white sauce
¾ cup grated cheddar cheese
4 eggs, separated
1 teaspoon sugar
salt and pepper to taste

WHITE SAUCE
1 stick margarine
¼ cup flour
1¼ cups milk

Trim cauliflower and cut into florets. Cook in boiling salted water until barely tender. Drain. Place cauliflower in a buttered shallow baking dish. To make white sauce, melt margarine in a heavy saucepan. Stir in flour. Cook 1 minute. Slowly add milk, stirring constantly. Stir and cook over medium heat until thick. Combine white sauce and cheese. Beat in egg yolks, sugar, salt, and pepper. Beat egg whites until stiff and fold into white sauce. Pour sauce over cauliflower. Bake at 350 degrees for 20 minutes or until sauce is firm.

Bootsie Clark
El Campo

Corn Casserole

1 stick margarine
1 small onion, chopped
1 small can green chilies, chopped
garlic salt to taste
salt and pepper to taste
1 8-ounce package cream cheese
3 cans vacuum-packed corn

Sauté onion and chilies in margarine. Season with salt, pepper, and garlic salt. Add cream cheese and melt, then add corn. Simmer to develop flavors (a crockpot works well).

Karen Lee
Mineral Wells

Corn Loaf

2 cups fresh corn, sliced from cob
1 cup peeled, chopped tomatoes
1 cup onions, chopped
1 cup bell pepper, chopped
2 teaspoons salt
⅛ teaspoon red pepper or to taste
1 cup yellow cornmeal
1 cup grated cheddar cheese
2 eggs, beaten
½ cup evaporated milk
½ cup water

My grandmother served slices of this with ham slices—as a sandwich. It's very good.

Combine corn, tomatoes, onions, bell pepper, salt, red pepper, cornmeal, and cheese. Mix well and let set for 30 minutes. Combine eggs, milk, and water and add to corn mixture. Thoroughly grease a 2-quart casserole dish or loaf pan. Bake at 375 degrees for 1 hour. Serve hot or cold.

Peggy Dunn
Fort Worth

Copper Carrots

3 cups cooked carrots
¾ cup oil
2 teaspoons prepared mustard
1 bell pepper, chopped
1 onion, chopped
1 cup brown sugar
1 can tomato soup

Mix all ingredients and store in covered dish in refrigerator. Serve cold.

Peggy Milner
Spring Branch

Jalapeño-Corn Casserole

1 cup uncooked rice
1 medium onion, chopped
1 medium bell pepper, chopped
1 cup celery, chopped
½ cup butter or margarine, melted
1 tablespoon sugar
1 or 2 large jalapeño peppers, chopped fine
2 17-ounce cans cream-style corn
1 cup shredded mild cheddar cheese

Cook rice according to package directions; set aside. Sauté onion, bell pepper, and celery in butter until vegetables are tender. Combine rice, sautéed vegetables, and remaining ingredients, stirring well. Spoon mixture into a lightly greased 12″ × 8″ × 2″ baking dish. Bake at 350 degrees for 40 to 45 minutes.

Eleanor Saunders
Dallas

Eggplant Casserole

1 pound ground chuck
½ cup onion, chopped
1 teaspoon salt
¼ teaspoon pepper
¼ teaspoon garlic powder
1 tablespoon parsley flakes
1 16-ounce can tomatoes
1 medium eggplant

This is a juicy casserole, so it's best served with cornbread or French bread to mop up the good juices.

Preheat oven to 350 degrees. Sauté ground chuck until lightly browned. Add onion and continue cooking until onion is soft. Remove from heat and stir in salt, pepper, garlic powder, and parsley flakes. Drain tomatoes, reserving liquid, and chop tomatoes to a coarse pulp. Wash eggplant and remove stem end. Do not peel. Slice eggplant crosswise in 1-inch-thick slices and arrange in layers in a 2- or 3-quart casserole dish so that top layer is fairly flat. Pour reserved tomato liquid over eggplant. Spread meat mixture over top. Spread tomato pulp over meat (like icing on a cake). Bake for 15 minutes. Cover and bake for 1 hour more. Serves 6.

Wanda Dickinson
Dallas

Green Bean Casserole

1 medium onion, diced
2 tablespoons margarine
2 tablespoons flour
2 tablespoons water
1 teaspoon salt
½ teaspoon black pepper
2 tablespoons lemon juice
2 No. 303 cans green beans, drained
1 cup sour cream
½ cup shredded cheddar cheese
½ cup dry bread crumbs

Sauté onion in margarine. Gradually stir in flour, water, salt, pepper, and lemon juice; simmer for 3 minutes. Add beans and sour cream. Place in a 2-quart casserole. Sprinkle with cheese and bread crumbs. Bake at 350 degrees for 30 minutes.

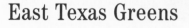

East Texas Greens

6 green onions, chopped
½ pound salt pork, scored
6 cups cold water
2 heaping tablespoons sugar
6 cups water
4 bunches turnip greens (or collard or mustard greens)

Combine onions and salt pork in pot with cold water. Bring to a boil, then cook for 30 minutes. Peel turnips. Wash greens, one leaf at a time, to remove all grit. Add to pot and bring to a boil, then lower heat and continue to boil gently for 1 hour and 45 minutes, covered. Serve with hot-water cornbread.

Iantha Pennil
Dallas

I grew up in Marshall in East Texas and every Sunday we had greens. Still do—it's a family tradition.

Okra Patties

1 pound okra, sliced or chopped fine
½ cup chopped onion
1 teaspoon salt
¼ teaspoon pepper
½ cup water
1 egg
½ cup flour
1 teaspoon baking powder
½ cup cornmeal
oil or bacon grease

Combine okra, onion, salt, pepper, water, and egg and mix well. Mix flour, baking powder, and cornmeal and add to okra mixture. Drop by tablespoons into hot oil or bacon grease and brown well over medium heat.

Betty Norton
Amarillo

This is the recipe used at the steak houses which have operated over the years in Lowake, a Concho County community. It's messy but worth it.

Lowake Onion Rings

onions
buttermilk
flour
salt

Slice onions and separate into rings. Dip in buttermilk, then in flour. Repeat. Deep-fry and sprinkle with salt.

Joe Michael Feist
Lancaster

Squash Patties

2 cups grated uncooked yellow squash
2 teaspoons grated onion
2 teaspoons sugar
½ teaspoon salt
⅛ teaspoon pepper
1 egg, beaten
¼ cup plus 2 tablespoons flour
2 tablespoons margarine

Combine squash, onion, sugar, salt, and pepper in bowl. Cover and let stand 30 minutes. Drain thoroughly. Add egg and flour, stirring well. Melt margarine in large skillet, drop squash mixture by tablespoons into hot margarine. Cook until golden brown, turning once.

Betty Cluck
Van

Mary's Squash Casserole

1 large onion, chopped
½ stick margarine
2 cups cooked yellow squash
2 cups crumbled cooked cornbread
1 can cream of chicken soup
salt and pepper to taste

Sauté onion in margarine. Combine with remaining ingredients and stir well. Pour into baking dish. Bake 20 to 40 minutes at 400 degrees.

Nan Smith
Carrollton

Fiesta Zucchini Squares

1 cup sliced carrots
1 cup chopped celery
4 eggs
4 cups sliced zucchini
½ cup chopped onion
½ cup grated cheddar cheese
2 ounces (1/2 can) chopped green chilies or more to taste
½ cup vegetable oil
½ teaspoon oregano
1 cup Bisquick

Cook carrots and celery for 5 minutes at high setting in the microwave or over high heat in a pan. Beat eggs slightly in a large mixing bowl. Add remaining ingredients, then add carrots and celery. Pour into an oiled 9″ × 13″ baking dish. Bake at 350 degrees about 40 minutes or until a toothpick comes out clean. Cut into squares to serve. (These freeze well and are good reheated.)

Mrs. James L. Boone
Bryan

Every since I was a little girl, I have loved the Sons of the Pioneers song "Tumbling Tumbleweeds." When I married, I found out from my husband, also a native Texan, that tumbleweeds are edible and high in iron. Being a pretty good cook (and a better eater), I decided I had to figure out a way to make tumbleweeds that would be not just palatable but delicious. This is the result.

Frazier Anderson is a brick collector. In addition to his extensive collection of bricks, he is a leading member of the National Brick Collectors Association.

Texas Tumbleweeds

In the late spring and early summer, when the tumbleweeds are first coming out, pull the young, tender weeds when they are about 4 to 5 inches high. Pull off the roots, wash tumbleweeds in a colander, and blanch.

Sauté some chopped onion in a little oil, then add a can of tomato paste and enough water to make a medium-thick sauce. Add salt, pepper, a pinch of sugar, garlic, hot pepper, and any other spices desired. Finally, add prepared tumbleweeds and simmer for a few minutes. Serve as a side dish or over a bed of rice, especially Spanish rice.

Ann Wilbourn
Clint

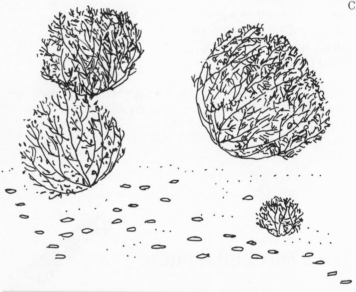

Tomato Gravy

2 fresh tomatoes, diced
1 tablespoon bacon drippings
1 teaspoon salt
1½ cups cold water
½ cup flour

Combine tomatoes, bacon drippings, and salt in skillet and cook covered over medium heat until tomatoes are soft. Pulverize with fork and let cook another 3 minutes.

Meanwhile combine cold water and flour in a shaker, cover, and shake vigorously. Pour over tomatoes, stirring constantly until thick. If thinner gravy is desired, add more water. Serve over hot biscuit halves. Serves 6.

Ollie M. and Frazier Anderson
Fort Worth

Baked Stuffed Tomato

1 medium tomato
1 tablespoon minced onion
2 tablespoons ground peanuts
⅛ teaspoon salt
1 slice cooked bacon, crumbled
2 tablespoons grated cheese, divided
1 teaspoon butter

Scoop out tomato pulp. Combine onion, ground peanuts, salt, bacon, and 1 tablespoon grated cheese; mix well. Spoon mixture into tomato shell, sprinkle with 1 tablespoon grated cheese, and dot with butter. Bake at 350 degrees for 25 minutes. Serves 2.

Margaret Schultz
Hereford

After I came to Hereford from California in 1983 to stay with my widowed father, he asked me to make cornbread and biscuits, which I had not made in about 25 years. My dad especially liked peanuts, but they hurt his gum and jaws, so I decided to grind some in the blender. I got the idea of putting peanut "powder" in various other goodies, too.

Hominy Olé

1 pound bacon, cut in pieces
1 cup chopped onion
2 cans hominy, drained
1 16-ounce can tomatoes, undrained
1 1¼-ounce package taco seasoning mix
1 cup grated cheese
dash of Tabasco sauce

Brown bacon and onion, add hominy, and sauté a few minutes. Drain off excess grease. Blend in tomatoes, taco seasoning mix, cheese, and Tabasco sauce. Heat thoroughly, stirring until cheese melts. Serves 6.

Peggy Busbee
Bedford

This recipe, which was my mother's, is at least sixty years old. We had this for supper on winter nights with fried chicken. If there was any left, she would flour it well after slicing and fry it for a meal the next day, or sometimes we just had it warmed over. Our grown children along with our grandchildren now have this for our Christmas Day brunch.

Grits Casserole

1½ cups uncooked grits
1½ teaspoons salt
6 cups boiling water
2 rolls garlic cheese, cut in small pieces
4 teaspoons savory salt or seasoning salt
12 drops Tabasco sauce or other hot pepper sauce
3 eggs, well beaten
1 stick margarine or butter

Pour grits into boiling water with salt added. Cook for 20 minutes, stirring constantly. (Be careful of grits popping up while cooking.) Remove from heat; add cheese, seasoning salt, and Tabasco sauce. Then add beaten eggs and stir well. Pour into buttered casserole dish and place cubes of margarine on top. Bake at 275 degrees until firm.

Sis Rich
Diboll

This yummy dish is much sought after and won't strain anyone's cooking skills.

Father Robert Williams has resurrected the age-old art of making sundials.

Monk's Beans

4 cans cooked black beans
2 cans whole tomatoes, cored
1 onion, chopped
2 garlic cloves, chopped
2 teaspoons ground cumin
2 tablespoons green peppercorns

Cook beans, tomatoes, and onion in a crockpot until tender. Add remaining ingredients 20 minutes before serving.

Fr. Robert Williams
Austin

Crider's Baked Beans

1 large onion, diced
1½ tablespoons Worcestershire sauce
½ teaspoon Tabasco sauce
1 teaspoon garlic powder
2 heaping tablespoons brown sugar
1½ teaspoons dry mustard
1 teaspoon vinegar
2 15½-ounce cans pork and beans
bacon strips
ham or bacon drippings

Cook onion, Worcestershire sauce, Tabasco sauce, garlic, brown sugar, dry mustard, and vinegar in a little water until onion is tender. Mix with beans and turn into a casserole dish. Cover with bacon strips and sprinkle with extra brown sugar and ham or bacon drippings. Bake 1 hour at 325 degrees. Serves 6.

Jan Thompson
Athens

Pinto Beans

3 pounds pinto beans
1 teaspoon oregano
1 large onion, chopped
3 to 4 tablespoons oil
2 large cloves garlic, minced
4 or 5 large bay leaves
1 teaspoon cumin
1 jalapeño pepper, chopped
1½ tablespoons salt
1 teaspoon chili powder
2 or 3 smoked pork hocks

Wash and soak beans in water 1 to 2 hours. Drain off water and set beans aside. In cooking pot, brown onion in oil until very browned. Add garlic and cook until onion is very dark brown. Add beans and remaining ingredients. Fill pot with water and cook slowly for at least one day (two is better). Chill beans and skim off the fat that has risen to the top. Reheat before serving.

Joan Bingham
Arlington

Texas Red Beans and Rice

2 pounds red kidney beans
8 smoked ham hocks
1 4½-ounce bottle smoke sauce
3 tablespoons chili powder
1 tablespoon pepper
1 tablespoon salt
4 tablespoons onion flakes
1 to 2 tablespoons ground cumin
dash of cayenne powder
2 cups uncooked rice
4 cups water

Soak beans overnight. Cook beans with ham hocks and spices for at least 6 hours over medium heat or until meat falls away from the bone. Remove bones and ham skin. Add a little water to thin beans if necessary. Cook rice about 45 minutes or until done. Mix with beans and serve.

Wendy Allen
Dublin

My grandmother was born in Iowa in 1857. She was widowed at a young age with two children and later moved to Kansas City. Then she came to Texas around 1904 for her health. She was a postmistress in Dixieland, Texas (located in Loving or Reeves County—it became a ghost town). In 1907 she married a rancher and cooked for the cowboys on the ranch. She lived to be 91 and died in Pecos in 1958.

Texas Best Baked Beans

4 slices bacon, cut into 1½-inch pieces
2 tablespoons chopped onion
2 tablespoons chopped bell pepper
1 21-ounce can pork and beans
2 tablespoons molasses
⅛ teaspoon hot pepper sauce

Fry bacon until crisp; set aside. Reserve 1 tablespoon drippings in pan. Sauté onion and bell pepper in drippings until tender. Combine with beans, molasses, and pepper sauce in a 1-quart casserole dish. Bake 30 minutes at 350 degrees. Top with bacon.

Nancy Noey
Normangee

My Grandmother's Ranch Beans

1 pound dried pinto beans
1 large onion, chopped
1 tablespoon chili powder
½ cup chopped ham or 2 slices bacon, chopped
salt and pepper to taste
1 16-ounce can tomatoes, undrained and mashed

Wash beans well and place in a large pan; cover with water and soak overnight. Drain and rinse. In a large pot combine beans, onion, chili powder, ham or bacon, and salt and pepper. Fill pan three-quarters full with water, covering all ingredients. Cook uncovered until beans are soft, adding water if necessary. When beans are soft, add tomatoes and cook until thick.

R. J. Barr
Fort Worth

Microwave Cottage Fries

3 medium Irish potatoes
1 large white onion, sliced
1 teaspoon black pepper
1 tablespoon dried parsley
¼ cup water
½ stick margarine

Wash potatoes and slice cottage-fry style. Layer all of the ingredients. Microwave approximately 12 minutes, stirring every 3 to 4 minutes. Serve with sour cream and chopped green onions.

LuDean Walston
Dallas

Devil-Fried Potatoes

4 tablespoons shortening
2 tablespoons mustard with horseradish
1 medium onion, chopped
5 or 6 medium potatoes, sliced thin
salt and pepper to taste

Melt shortening in a heavy iron skillet with a tight-fitting lid. Add mustard with horseradish and mix. Add chopped onion and cook slightly. Add potatoes and salt and pepper, turning all ingredients several times. Cover and cook. Turn occasionally. (Some potatoes will be brown and some white.)

Beatrice Nagle
Irving

In 1945 as we pulled a house trailer from California to Texas, we spent the night in White Sands National Park, New Mexico. I fixed this recipe of Devil-Fried Potatoes—it's great for outdoor meals.

Bohemian Potato Dumplings

3 large Irish potatoes, peeled and grated fine
2½ to 3 cups flour
1 teaspoon salt
2 teaspoons baking powder
½ pound bacon, diced
1 small onion, chopped

Grate potatoes and pour off excess water. Add 2 cups flour, baking powder, and salt. Stir well to form a soft dough, adding more flour as needed for dough to hold together when dropped in boiling water. Drop dumplings by heaping tablespoonfuls into large pot of boiling water and boil for approximately 12 minutes. Drain well. In a large iron skillet, fry bacon pieces and onion together until bacon is done and onions are slightly brown. Add dumplings and stir gently until coated and heated through.

Irene Goedrich
Baytown

This recipe was given to me by my maternal grandmother, who came to America in the early 1900s from Czechoslovakia. My mother served it to our family often when I was growing up, with either pork chops or pork loin roast, sauerkraut, and rye bread.

Spanish Rice

1 cup uncooked rice
oil for frying
1 medium onion, diced
1 medium bell pepper, diced
1 can Ro-tel tomatoes, diced
1 small can tomato sauce
salt to taste
½ teaspoon red pepper
2½ to 3 cups water

Fry rice in oil until golden brown, then add onion and bell pepper. Fry until onions turn brown, stirring constantly. Add tomatoes, tomato sauce, salt, red pepper, and water. Let simmer, stirring occasionally until rice is tender and most of the juice is absorbed. If rice is still firm, add a little more water.

Linda Ray
Bryan

This is a great side dish that goes well with most meats. It's especially good served with barbecued chicken, brisket, or pork chops. If you're cooking for a large crowd, the recipe can be doubled or tripled. This is my own original recipe and it's a winner at our house.

Country Rice, Brenda's Style

1½ cups rice, cooked, rinsed, and drained
3 tablespoons cooking oil
1 medium onion, chopped
1 medium bell pepper, chopped
1 15-ounce can mixed vegetables
2 teaspoons parsley flakes
¼ cup soy sauce
¾ cup water

Heat cooking oil in large skillet. Add drained rice and chopped onion. Stir-fry for 1 minute. Add chopped bell pepper, mixed vegetables, parsley flakes, soy sauce, and water. Stir-fry for 2 minutes longer.

Brenda Sanders
Whitney

Tarragon Rice

1 stick margarine
1 cup chopped onions
1 cup chopped celery
1 cup chopped bell pepper
1 teaspoon dried tarragon
1 cup uncooked rice
2 cans beef consommé

Combine margarine, onions, celery, bell pepper, tarragon, and rice together and sauté. Add beef consommé to mixture and transfer to a baking dish. Bake for 1 hour at 400 degrees, stirring occasionally.

Rosie Devillier Hearn
Winnie

Rosie Devillier Hearn is the daughter of Olide Coulon Devillier, who was voted "Pioneer Rice Farmer of the Year" by the Rice Association of Texas in Winnie. Devillier has been farming rice for the past seventy-five years.

Sweet Potato Soufflé

SOUFFLÉ
3 cups cooked mashed sweet potatoes
1 stick margarine
1 teaspoon vanilla
2 eggs
1 cup sugar
pinch of salt

TOPPING
½ cup chopped pecans
1 cup brown sugar
⅓ cup flour
½ cup shredded coconut
⅔ cup melted margarine

Beat soufflé ingredients together well with electric mixer. Place in greased ovenproof dish. Spread with topping and bake at 350 degrees for 30 minutes.

Marilyn and Milton Watts
Jefferson

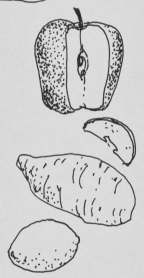

Candied Sweet Potatoes

4 medium sweet potatoes
1 cup pineapple juice
1 cup brown sugar
¼ cup white sugar
3 tablespoons butter
½ teaspoon cinnamon

Bake sweet potatoes. Peel and slice lengthwise; place in a greased casserole dish. Combine remaining ingredients and boil 10 minutes. Pour over potatoes and bake at 350 degrees until syrup is thick.

Billie Jean Hepp
Van

Yams and Apples

6 medium yams
5 Jonathan apples, peeled
1 cup sugar
2 cups water
3 tablespoons cornstarch
juice of ½ lemon
¼ pound butter

Boil yams slowly until partially done; cool and peel. Slice yams and apples alternately into a buttered ovenproof dish, beginning with apples. Combine and cook remaining ingredients until thickened. Pour over apples and yams. Bake at 350 degrees for 1 hour. Serves 8.

Ruth Dowlen
Wichita Falls

EGGS & CHEESE

About 30 years ago, I went deer hunting on a ranch in South Texas. An old vaquero who had worked on the ranch for years was called on to cook for us during the hunt. When we roused up around four o'clock in the morning to get ready for a sun-up hunt, the old ranch hand had prepared migas for our breakfast—it was one of those moments in life that I'll always remember.

Charlie's Egg Scramble

3 eggs
3 tablespoons salsa
2 tablespoons dry sherry
2 tablespoons margarine
2 tablespoons olive oil
¼ cup chopped onion
½ cup chopped bell pepper
½ cup chopped ham
1 cup sliced mushrooms
½ cup shredded cheese (mozzarella, cheddar, or Monterey Jack)

Break eggs into medium mixing bowl and add salsa and sherry. Blend together and set aside. In a 10-inch frypan, heat margarine and olive oil. Add onion and bell pepper and steam until onions are translucent. Add ham and mushrooms and cook slowly. Add cheese; when cheese is melted, add egg mixture. Cook over moderate heat until eggs are firm. Serves 2.

Charles Schultz
Kerrville

Sam's Migas Supreme

¼ pound butter
¼ cup chopped onions
2 corn tortillas per person, cut into ¼-inch pieces
2½ eggs per person, beaten
1 small can chopped green chilies
1 small jar mild picante sauce
1 cup shredded cheddar cheese
1 chopped tomato

Sauté chopped onions in part of the butter until clear but not brown. Add more butter and add corn tortillas. Stir until tortillas are covered with butter and wilted. Add eggs, green chilies, and a generous portion of picante sauce. Stir until eggs are soft-scrambled. Transfer egg mixture to large microwave-safe platter. Cover mixture with cheese and heat in microwave just long enough to melt cheese; don't overcook. Remove from microwave and garnish with tomato. Serve with small smoked sausages, bacon, or chorizo; a dish of heated picante sauce; or English muffins and raspberry jam (a gringo touch).

Sam Tayloe
El Paso

German-Fried Potatoes and Eggs

5 medium potatoes
oil for frying
12 eggs
milk
salt and pepper to taste

Peel and cut potatoes into bite-size chunks. Fry in hot oil until slightly brown. Remove from skillet and drain off excess oil. Scramble eggs with milk and salt and pepper. Mix eggs with fried potatoes and return to skillet. Cook until eggs are done. Serves 8.

Julie Morris
Van Alstyne

My father's parents immigrated to Dallas from Germany as teenagers in the late 1880s and settled in the German neighborhood of East Dallas. They later married and raised five children in that same neighborhood. This recipe was a favorite Sunday-night supper for my father, Frank Schulz, Jr.

Special Eggs

8 eggs, beaten
1 tablespoon margarine
1 cup cubed ham
1½ cups grated Colby or cheddar cheese
1½ cups white sauce
1 tablespoon fresh or freeze-dried chives
paprika
cayenne pepper (optional)

WHITE SAUCE
3 tablespoons margarine
3 tablespoons flour
1½ cups milk
salt and pepper to taste

In a skillet cook beaten eggs in margarine until just partially set. Spread eggs in an even layer over bottom of lightly greased 8½″ × 11″ baking dish. To make white sauce, melt margarine in saucepan, add flour, and stir until well mixed. Slowly add milk, stirring constantly until thickened to gravy consistency. Sprinkle ham evenly over eggs, followed by 1 cup of the cheese, white sauce, remaining cheese, chives, paprika, and cayenne pepper. (At this point the dish may be covered with foil and refrigerated overnight.) Bake at 350 degrees for 25 to 30 minutes or until cheese is melted and dish is bubbling. Serve immediately.

June Jordan
Caddo Mills

This dish is especially good for holiday breakfasts because it can be made ahead and baked with biscuits while you enjoy your family or guests. It also makes a great quick supper.

John Wayne Casserole

2 cans green chilies
1 pound Monterey Jack cheese, grated
1 pound cheddar cheese, grated
4 eggs, separated
⅔ cup evaporated milk
1 tablespoon flour
½ teaspoon salt
⅛ teaspoon pepper
2 medium tomatoes

My mother gave me this recipe a long time ago—John Wayne is said to have liked it a lot.

Remove seeds from chilies and split. In a large bowl combine chilies and cheeses. Turn into a well-buttered 2-quart casserole dish. In a large bowl beat egg whites until they form stiff peaks. In another bowl, combine egg yolks, milk, flour, salt, and pepper until well blended. Fold egg whites into egg yolk mixture, then pour over cheese mixture. Use a fork to separate cheese and allow mixture to soak through. Arrange sliced tomatoes on top. Bake at 350 degrees about 30 minutes or until knife inserted in middle comes out clean.

Lila Markham
Dumas

Sour Cream Enchiladas

vegetable oil for frying
1 cup chopped onion
2 cups tomato sauce
1 10-ounce can mild enchilada sauce
2 4-ounce cans chopped green chilies
12 corn tortillas
8 ounces Monterey Jack cheese, cut into 24 strips
1 pint sour cream

Heat 1 teaspoon oil in a sauté pan. Add onion and fry until it begins to brown. Add tomato sauce, enchilada sauce, and chilies. Bring to a boil and cook 1 minute. In a skillet, heat ½ cup oil. Dip tortillas in hot oil one at a time to soften. Drain on paper towels. Place one strip of cheese, 1 tablespoon sauce mixture, and 1 tablespoon sour cream in center of each tortilla. Roll and place in a baking dish, folded side down. Top each tortilla with a strip of cheese and 1 teaspoon sour cream. Pour remaining mixture over tortillas. Bake at 350 degrees for 20 minutes.

Rose England
Groom

Baked Chiles Rellenos

2 4-ounce cans whole green chilies
8 ounces Monterey Jack cheese
4 eggs, beaten
⅓ cup skim milk
½ cup flour
½ teaspoon baking powder
½ teaspoon salt
½ cup shredded cheddar cheese

Drain peppers, cut in half lengthwise, and remove seeds. Cut Monterey Jack cheese into strips to fit inside peppers. Wrap each pepper around a strip of cheese and arrange in a greased 10″ × 6″ × 2″ baking dish. Mix eggs and milk. Beat in flour, baking powder, and salt. Pour over peppers. Sprinkle with cheddar cheese. Bake at 350 degrees for 30 minutes. Cut into 2-inch squares and serve immediately.

Karen Hillis
Rowlett

Quiche Laredo

1 7-ounce can jalapeño peppers, drained and sliced
5 ounces cheddar cheese, grated
5 ounces Monterey Jack cheese, grated
6 eggs at room temperature, slightly beaten
2 tablespoons Pace picante sauce

Coat a glass pie pan with nonstick spray. Sprinkle jalapeños evenly over bottom of pan, followed by grated cheeses. Combine beaten eggs and picante sauce and add to cheese mixture. Let set for 10 to 12 minutes. Bake at 350 degrees 30 to 35 minutes. Cool at least 30 minutes before cutting into slices for bite-size pieces (for appetizer). For the faint-hearted, substitute mushrooms and ham for the jalapeños and use grated Swiss cheese instead of Monterey Jack.

Mrs. W. Tom Ridlehuber
Waco

After spending most of my life in Austin, I do know a tiny bit about what Texans find tasty, and this recipe seems to please both family and friends back home as well as the Dutch who have enjoyed it. It originates from a Dutch recipe I got from my mother-in-law, but I've changed it around considerably to make it easier to make and tastier as well.

Tineke's Tomato and Onion Quiche

CRUST
1½ cups flour
1 egg
2 tablespoons cold water
scant ½ cup butter or margarine

FILLING
2 tablespoons butter or margarine
3 cups onions, sliced thin
1 16-ounce can tomatoes, drained and sliced
4 eggs
¾ cup cream
1½ cups grated Swiss or Gouda cheese
salt and pepper to taste

Combine crust ingredients and mix together quickly. Refrigerate. Meanwhile, to make filling, melt butter in a deep skillet and cook onions until soft. Press dough for crust into an 8½-inch spring-form pan or a pie pan. (The pan should be three-fourths covered.) Spread cooked onions evenly over the bottom of the crust and top with tomatoes. Beat eggs together with cream and grated cheese; season with salt and pepper. Pour this mixture over the onions and tomatoes, covering well. Press sides of crust gently down, if needed, to form an even and attractive edge. Bake at 400 degrees for about 1 hour or until done.

Karen Call
Dordrecht
The Netherlands

Macaroni and Two Cheeses

1 cup elbow macaroni
2 tablespoons margarine
2 tablespoons flour
1 tablespoon grated onion
¼ teaspoon dry mustard
1 teaspoon salt (optional)
⅛ teaspoon black pepper
1 cup milk
1½ cups grated sharp cheddar cheese
1½ cups grated aged Vermont cheddar cheese
¾ cup bread crumbs (mixed with 4 tablespoons melted
    margarine)

Cook macaroni, then drain. Melt margarine and add flour, grated onion, mustard, salt, and pepper. Stir until smooth, adding milk gradually. Cook over medium heat until smooth and thick. Add 2¼ cups cheese and cooked macaroni. Mix well. Pour into a 1½-quart baking dish. Sprinkle remaining cheese over top, then spread with bread crumbs. Bake at 375 degrees for 25 to 30 minutes. (This is easy to double and can be prepared the night before and then baked the next day.)

Helen Tullis
El Paso

Macaroni and Cheese Custard

3 cups cooked macaroni
6 ounces grated cheddar cheese
¾ cup grated Parmesan cheese
½ cup grated or chopped onion
6 eggs
½ cup half-and-half
1 cup sour cream
½ teaspoon nutmeg
salt and pepper to taste

Place macaroni in a large bread pan or heat-resistant bowl. Add cheeses and onion; mix well.

In a 4- to 6-cup mixing bowl, blend together remaining ingredients. Pour over the macaroni mixture and stir well, making sure the custard mixture penetrates all the way to the bottom.

Wrap pan in a double thickness of aluminum foil, shiny sides together; cover the top with a double thickness also. Punch dime-size holes in the top cover. Place in outdoor cooker and cook for about 1 hour or until a toothpick inserted in the middle comes out clean. (This recipe will work just as well in an oven, but the cooking time will vary.)

Jim and Beverly Lee
Reagan Wells

Mesquite imparts a wonderful flavor to meat, poultry, and fish dishes. We also love vegetables and pasta dishes prepared over mesquite fires. Here's one of our favorites.

Jim and Beverly Lee, who call themselves "The Hummers," are woodturners. They create useful wooden objects from old pieces of wood.

POULTRY

My maternal grandmother had eighteen grandchildren, who all thought they were her favorite. Sunday dinner at her house always meant fried chicken (in a black skillet, of course), creamed potatoes, fresh green beans, homemade chow-chow, bread and butter pickles, fried okra, and biscuits (she made biscuits three times a day).

This is the way chicken was cooked in Jefferson Davis's time. The chicken will be cooked to the bone and there will be no pink meat.

Fried Chicken

2 eggs
¾ cup milk
1½ cups flour
1 teaspoon salt
½ teaspoon pepper
½ teaspoon sage
2 chickens, cut up and skinned
shortening for frying

GRAVY
⅓ to ½ cup pan drippings
½ cup flour
2½ to 3 cups milk
salt and pepper to taste

Beat eggs and milk in a pie dish. Mix flour and seasonings in a separate dish. Dredge chicken in flour mixture, dip in egg batter, then in flour mixture again. Place on paper towels and let set for 15 minutes. Meanwhile heat a cast-iron skillet and add shortening to a depth of 1 inch. When heated to about 350 degrees (a bread cube takes 1 minute to brown), add chicken. Cover and cook 10 minutes or until well browned. (Reduce heat if chicken is browning too fast.) Uncover, turn once, and cook 5 more minutes. To make gravy, stir flour into pan drippings and cook until light brown. Add milk and bring to a simmer. Simmer 5 minutes. Season with salt and pepper.

Judie Jones
Arlington

Southern Fried Chicken

chicken, cut up into serving pieces
fine cracker crumbs
4 heaping teaspoons butter

Place chicken in a pressure cooker and cook for 10 for 20 minutes. (This will tenderize the meat and prevent stringiness. Just boiling it, however, will make it dry and tough.) Remove chicken from pressure cooker and dust lightly with cracker crumbs. In a large frying pan melt butter over medium heat. Pan-fry about 5 minutes or until light brown, turning frequently. Serve immediately.

Lela Budwine
Amarillo

Country-Fried Chicken Strips

1 cup flour
2 teaspoons garlic salt
2 teaspoons pepper
1 teaspoon paprika
½ teaspoon poultry seasoning
½ cup milk
1 egg, slightly beaten
6 to 8 deboned chicken breasts, cut into strips
vegetable oil for frying

Combine first five ingredients and set aside. Combine milk and egg, mixing well. Roll chicken in flour mixture, then dip in milk and egg batter, and roll again in flour mixture. Heat 1 inch of oil in a large skillet. Add chicken strips and fry until golden brown, turning once.

Beverly Fair
Fort Worth

Texas Golden Chicken Breast

1 stick butter (not margarine or cooking oil)
1 tablespoon olive oil
1 cup flour
1 tablespoon crushed rosemary
3 tablespoons grated Parmesan cheese
4 split boneless, skinless chicken breasts
2 cups fine-grated croutons
2 eggs, beaten well
2 tablespoons water

In a large heavy skillet, heat butter and olive oil over low heat. In a separate bowl combine flour, rosemary, and cheese and mix well. Dampen chicken breast. Roll in flour mixture, then eggs, then croutons. Cook in butter four minutes per side. Serve with a white sauce or with milk gravy.

Mary Haston
Wortham

I never was good at cooking fried chicken, so I thought I would experiment with some chicken breast. I have always loved the taste of butter, so I came up with this recipe. What we like about it is that the chicken breast always comes out moist and tender.

Stuffed Chicken Legs

½ pound chopped mushrooms
1 large red bell pepper, chopped
1 large green bell pepper, chopped
2 large cloves garlic, minced fine
⅓ cup chopped onion
1 large stalk celery, minced fine
1 teaspoon salt
8 ounces frozen chopped spinach
½ teaspoon oregano
¼ teaspoon basil
2 tablespoons lemon juice
4 large leg quarters, washed and dried
¼ cup butter, melted
4 slices Swiss cheese

In a large bowl mix chopped mushrooms, red bell pepper, green bell pepper, garlic, onion, celery, salt, spinach, oregano, basil, and lemon juice and set aside. Carefully loosen skin on chicken quarters, cut away excess external fat, and stuff loosely with vegetable and herb mixture. Bake at 350 degrees for 35 to 40 minutes. Brush with butter and brown underneath a broiler for up to 3 minutes. Cover each piece of chicken with one slice of cheese.

Carol Renee Queen
Port Arthur

This recipe came from Mommee's Sunday school class luncheons. It makes an especially good low-fat, low-cholesterol meal when served with a tossed green salad and garlic bread.

Chicken-Rice Casserole

1 cup brown rice, uncooked
1 cup water
1 can cream of celery soup
1 soup can water
½ cup chopped red and green bell peppers, onion, and celery (combined)
1 package dry onion soup mix (or less to taste)
4 chicken breasts, skinned

Spray casserole dish with nonstick spray. Layer all ingredients except chicken in order listed, ending with onion soup mix. Top with chicken breasts. Cover with foil and cook at 350 degrees for 1 hour or until chicken is tender. Serves 6 to 8.

Doris Sutton
Whitesboro

Poppyseed Chicken

4 to 5 chicken breasts
2 cans cream of chicken soup
8 ounces sour cream
2 cups seasoned Pepperidge Farm stuffing
2 tablespoons poppyseeds
1 stick margarine, melted

Boil chicken and cut up. Place chicken in a buttered 13″ × 9″ ovenproof dish. Mix soup and sour cream and pour over chicken. Sprinkle with seasoned stuffing and poppyseeds. Pour on melted butter. Bake at 350 degrees for 30 to 40 minutes or until bubbly.

Donna Uehlinger
Portland

Pollo Flautas

3 tablespoons margarine
¼ cup flour
¼ teaspoon salt
1 cup chicken broth
1 tablespoon lemon juice
1 tablespoon parsley
1 teaspoon grated onion
dash each of paprika, nutmeg, and pepper
1½ cups cooked chicken, diced fine
corn tortillas
vegetable oil for deep-frying

AVOCADO SAUCE
2 avocados, peeled and mashed
½ cup sour cream
1 teaspoon lemon juice
¼ teaspoon onion salt
10 drops hot pepper sauce

In a saucepan, combine margarine, flour, salt, and chicken broth. Cook and stir until thick. Then add lemon juice, parsley, onion, spices, and chicken. Place 1 tablespoon chicken mixture in center of a corn tortilla and roll up; secure with a toothpick. Deep-fry in vegetable oil for 1 to 2 minutes or until crisp. Serve with sour cream and/or Avocado Sauce.

Vanyelle Williams
Arlington

Texas Pecan Country Chicken

2 pounds whole chicken breasts, boned and skinned
¾ teaspoon salt
½ teaspoon pepper
2 tablespoons butter or margarine
8 ounces fresh mushrooms, chopped
½ small onion, diced (or 6 chopped green onions)
1 4-ounce package cream cheese, softened
1 tablespoon Dijon mustard
1 tablespoon snipped fresh thyme (or 1 teaspoon dried thyme)
1½ cups fine-chopped pecans
1 cup fine bread crumbs
¼ cup minced fresh parsley
½ cup melted butter or margarine

On a hard surface, with a meat mallet pound chicken to a thickness of ¼ inch. Sprinkle with salt and pepper; set aside. In small skillet, melt butter. Add mushrooms and onion and sauté until tender; cool. Mix with cream cheese, mustard, and thyme. Divide into four equal portions and spread on each piece of chicken. Fold over ends and roll up, pressing edges to seal. Mix pecans, bread crumbs, and parsley in a bowl. Dip chicken into melted butter, then into pecan mixture, turning to coat. Place on greased baking sheet, seam side down. Bake at 350 degrees 35 minutes or until done. Serve with rice. Makes 4 servings.

Dolores Booher
Irving

Donita's Chicken and Dumplings

4 tablespoons shortening
4 tablespoons flour
2 teaspoons salt
1 cup milk
1 cup chicken stock or bouillon
2 teaspoons chopped onion
1½ to 2 cups diced cooked chicken

DUMPLINGS
1 cup sifted flour
1½ teaspoons double-acting baking powder
½ teaspoon salt
2 tablespoons melted shortening
½ cup milk

Melt shortening in Dutch oven and blend in flour and salt. Add milk and stock. Cook over low heat until smooth and thick. Stir in onion and chicken and blend well. To make dumplings, combine dry ingredients with melted shortening and milk. Blend enough to moisten. Drop from teaspoon into hot chicken mixture. Cover tightly and cook for 15 minutes over medium heat without removing cover. (For puffy, fluffy dumplings, don't peek while they are cooking.) Makes 4 to 6 servings.

Donita Johnston
Slaton

Chicken 'n Feather Dumplings

1 4-pound chicken, cut into serving pieces
1 tablespoon salt

FEATHER DUMPLINGS
2 cups flour
1 teaspoon salt
4 teaspoons baking powder
¼ teaspoon black pepper
1 egg, well beaten
3 tablespoons butter, melted
⅔ cup milk

GRAVY
3 tablespoons flour
1 cup milk
salt and pepper to taste

In a large, heavy pot with a tight-fitting lid, place chicken and salt and cover with water. Bring to a boil, cover, and simmer for 1 hour; remove cover during last 30 minutes of cooking. Chicken should be tender but not falling away from the bone, and broth should be reduced to 1 quart. Remove chicken from pot and keep warm. To make dumplings, mix dry ingredients together. Add egg, melted butter, and milk to make a stiff batter. Drop by teaspoons into boiling chicken broth. Cover tightly and cook for 18 minutes. Place chicken on a large platter or 9″ × 13″ casserole dish. Remove dumplings with a slotted spoon and place on top of chicken. To make gravy, add flour to milk to form a paste. Add to pot and cook until thickened. Season with salt and pepper. Pour over chicken and dumplings. Serves 8.

Leila Doris Kelley
Valentine

Leila Kelley is the postmaster of Valentine, a tiny town in the West Texas desert. She handles all the cards that pour in around Valentine's Day from people everywhere wanting their valentines to be mailed with a Valentine postmark.

This recipe has been in my family for six generations. Abrilla Walker Guyton was famous for her dumplings. Her father, James Walker, Jr., fought in the Battle of San Jacinto. Her grandfather, James Walker, Sr., came to Texas with Stephen F. Austin's Old Three Hundred.

Family Secret Chicken and Dumplings

1 stewing chicken
salt to taste
water

DUMPLINGS
2½ cups flour
1 teaspoon baking powder
¼ teaspoon baking soda
½ teaspoon salt
¼ teaspoon black pepper
½ cup shortening or chicken fat
¼ cup sour milk
½ cup water
½ cup cold sweet milk

Cut up, salt, and boil chicken. Remove from broth. To make dumplings, sift all dry ingredients in a sifter. Cut shortening into dry ingredients. Add sour milk and water. Roll out to a thickness of ¼ inch and cut into strips. Drop into boiling chicken stock, cover, and cook 10 minutes. Pour cold sweet milk over the dumplings to set them. Serve with stewed chicken.

Georgia Jane Grubb Creel
San Antonio

Patti's Mexican Chicken Casserole

24 corn tortillas
1 3- to 4-pound chicken
1 4-ounce can chopped green chilies (or less for milder dish)
1 can cream of chicken soup
1 can cream of mushroom soup
1 cup chicken broth, reserved from cooked chicken
1 large onion, chopped fine
1 10-ounce package Kraft Sharp Cracker Barrel cheese, grated

Tear tortillas into dollar-size pieces. Cook and bone chicken, reserving chicken broth. Mix together remaining ingredients except cheese. In a greased 9″ × 13″ baking dish, alternate layers of tortilla pieces, cooked chicken, soup mixture, and cheese. Repeat until ingredients are all used, ending with cheese. Bake at 350 degrees for 30 to 45 minutes or until bubbly and cheese is melted. Bake at least 10 minutes more before serving.

Patti Cornett
Mount Calm

Dieter's Chicken Delight

4 medium white potatoes
3 large carrots
3 ribs celery
1 large white onion
1 teaspoon salt
½ teaspoon black pepper
1 14½-ounce can Swanson chicken broth
4 chicken breasts, skinned
paprika to taste
½ teaspoon each of sage, thyme, and oregano
2 envelopes McCormick's Lite Chicken Gravy mix
1 cup cold water

Pare vegetables and cut into 1-inch pieces. Place in a roaster and add salt and pepper and chicken broth. Spray a skillet with non-stick spray and quickly brown chicken breasts. Sprinkle with paprika. Lay chicken breasts on top of vegetables and simmer covered until tender. Add herbs. Blend gravy mix with cold water and add to simmering stew. Stir carefully and simmer about 1 minute or until gravy thickens.

Ruth Haggerton
Sherman

Chicken Spaghetti

1 large hen or fryer
salt and pepper
2 to 3 cups chopped celery
1 large onion, chopped
1 large green bell pepper, chopped
2 sticks margarine, melted
2 cans cream of mushroom soup
1 can cream of chicken soup
1 16-ounce package spaghetti

Boil hen or fryer in a large amount of water, seasoned to taste. Remove meat from bones and reserve stock. Sauté celery, onion, and bell pepper in margarine. Add boned chicken and soups and mix well. Cook spaghetti in reserved stock and add to chicken mixture. Top with sliced ripe olives, pimientos, slivered almonds, grated cheese, or sliced mushrooms (or a combination).

Edna Nelson
Shreveport, Louisiana

This recipe was my father-in-law's, the late Will White, who was from Sulphur Springs, Hopkins County, Texas. He said most people there in Depression days made this stew with rabbit or squirrel and cooked it in an iron washpot. At times the neighbors would gather for what they called a "stew out" and each one would bring a can of whatever they had and just dump it into the pot.

Cheddar and Green Chili Chicken

3 tablespoons flour
1 tablespoon chili powder
2 teaspoons salt
1 teaspoon cumin
1 frying chicken, cut into serving pieces
½ cup chopped celery
½ cup chopped onion
1 clove garlic, chopped
1 small can whole green chilies
¾ cup chicken broth
½ cup sour cream
1 cup shredded cheddar cheese
cooked noodles or rice

Mix flour, chili powder, salt, and cumin in paper bag. Shake chicken pieces in flour mixture until well coated. Place celery, onion, and garlic into bottom of casserole dish. Layer chicken on top of vegetables. Cut green chilies into 1-inch pieces and arrange over chicken pieces. Pour chicken broth into casserole, cover, and bake at 350 degrees for 45 minutes. Remove chicken from casserole and stir in sour cream. Replace chicken and top with cheese. Bake uncovered for an additional 5 to 10 minutes or until cheese melts. Serve over noodles or rice.

Kathy Jo Gamelin
Houston

Hopkins County Stew

2 chicken breasts, split
1 No. 2 can tomatoes, chopped
1 No. 2 can whole-kernel corn
2 medium onions, chopped
1 bell pepper, chopped
3 medium potatoes, chopped
3 ribs celery, chopped
salt to taste

In stewpot simmer chicken in water to cover until chicken is tender. Remove chicken and set aside. Strain broth and return to pot. Add vegetables and enough water to cover. Simmer until vegetables are tender. Bone and skin chicken and cut into bite-size pieces. Add to vegetables and return to simmer. Serve in soup bowls with cornbread. (This is even better reheated the next day.)

Emma White
Cleburne

Chicken Cacciatore

⅓ cup olive oil
4½ pounds chicken pieces, skinned
1 large onion, diced
1 medium green bell pepper, sliced
2 cloves garlic, minced
2 8-ounce cans tomato sauce
½ teaspoon pepper
¼ teaspoon thyme
2 teaspoons salt
1 28-ounce can tomatoes, cut into pieces
¼ cup red wine
½ teaspoon allspice
¼ teaspoon Italian seasoning

In Dutch oven brown chicken in olive oil. Remove chicken and set aside. Sauté onion and bell pepper about 5 minutes. Add remaining ingredients. Stir well. Return chicken to pot, bring to a boil, cover, and simmer about 40 minutes.

Frederick H. Anderson
Fort Worth

Mary Louise's Chicken Enchiladas

1 white onion, chopped
vegetable oil
1 package cream cheese
1 chicken, cooked and cubed
1 package flour tortillas
1 package Monterey Jack cheese, grated
½ pint whipping cream

Sauté onion in a small amount of oil. When onions are transparent, add cream cheese and cubed chicken. Stir until cheese is softened and well mixed. Put about ¼ cup of chicken mixture on each flour tortilla and roll. Place in a greased casserole dish. Generously cover rolled enchiladas with grated cheese. Pour whipping cream over enchiladas and cover with aluminum foil. Bake at 300 to 350 degrees for 30 minutes.

Michael White
Bryan

My mother gave me this recipe before I went off to college at Texas Tech University.

Lou's Mexican Chicken Casserole

2 cans cream of chicken soup
1 can chicken broth
1 small can chopped green chilies
1 medium package plain Doritos, crushed
1 bunch green onions, chopped
3 cans boneless chicken meat, shredded
1 small package shredded cheddar cheese
1 small package Monterey Jack cheese

Mix together chicken soup, chicken broth, and green chilies. In a large ovenproof casserole layer half the Doritos, half the onions, half the chicken, and half the cheese. Repeat, ending with a layer of Doritos. Pour soup mixture over top. Bake at 325 degrees about 30 minutes or until bubbly. Serves 10 to 12.

Lou Banner
Weston

Homemade Chicken Pot Pie

1 fryer, cut up
1 onion, sliced thin
½ cup chopped celery
1½ teaspoons salt
1½ teaspoons pepper
2 cups water
1 cup small pearl onions
1 cup cubed raw potatoes
1 cup cubed raw carrots
¼ cup flour
½ cup milk
1 cup English peas
unbaked pie crust

Boil chicken with onion, celery, salt, pepper, and water. Remove chicken from broth, skin and bone, and cut into chunks. In a saucepan heat 2 cups broth and add pearl onions, potatoes, and carrots. Cover and cook until tender but crisp. Remove vegetables with a slotted spoon. To the saucepan add broth to make 2 cups. Blend flour with milk and stir into broth; bring to a boil. Add cooked vegetables, English peas, and chicken. Pour into a large baking dish and top with pie crust. Cook at 425 degrees about 25 to 30 minutes or until crust is a golden brown. Serves 8.

Ann Kimbrough
Grand Saline

Slow-Cooker Dressing

1 cup butter or margarine
2 cups chopped onion
2 cups chopped celery
¼ cup minced parsley
6 cups slightly dry white bread
6 cups crumbled cornbread
1 teaspoon baking powder
1 teaspoon poultry seasoning
1½ teaspoons salt
2 teaspoons sage
½ teaspoon black pepper
4 cups broth
2 eggs, well beaten

Microwave onion, celery, and parsley in margarine. Mix white bread, cornbread, baking powder, and seasonings. Pour vegetable mixture over bread mixture. Pour broth over bread mixture. Add eggs and mix together well. Pack lightly in a 3½- to 4½-quart slow cooker. Cover and cook on high heat for 30 minutes. Reduce heat to low and cook 5 to 6 hours. (To bake in oven, bake 1 hour at 350 degrees.)

Cleo Howard
Temple

Old-Fashioned Dumplings

1½ cups flour
2 teaspoons baking powder
½ teaspoon salt
½ cup chicken broth
2 tablespoons vegetable oil
2 quarts broth or soup

Combine flour, baking powder, and salt. Add chicken broth and oil, stirring until dry ingredients are moistened. Turn dough onto a floured surface and form a ball. Then roll dough to a thickness of 1/16 inch. Cut into 5″ × 1″ strips. Drop dumplings into boiling broth; cover and cook 15 minutes or until dumplings are tender. Serves 8. (Note: Cooked chicken can be added to dumpling mixture if desired.)

DLee Poteet
Shepherd

This recipe has been used on offshore oil rigs to feed crews of 30 or more at one time.

Barbecued Turkey Breast Tenderloins

2 whole turkey tenderloins
6 slices bacon
½ onion, chopped
vegetable oil
1 cup catsup
¾ cup water
1 tablespoon Worcestershire sauce
1 teaspoon lemon juice
2 teaspoons sugar
½ teaspoon prepared mustard
salt and pepper to taste

Wrap each tenderloin with 3 slices of bacon; secure with tooth-picks. Cook onion in oil; then add remaining ingredients and cook slowly for 30 minutes. Barbecue turkey over medium-hot coals, basting frequently with sauce and turning once or twice. Pierce with a fork to test for doneness.

Fred, Penny, and Ady Stiles
Fort Worth

Country Sausage

1 pound ground turkey
½ cup fresh bread crumbs
2 cloves garlic, chopped fine
1 teaspoon thyme
1 teaspoon sage
½ teaspoon marjoram
½ teaspoon salt
½ teaspoon fresh-ground pepper
2 tablespoons safflower oil

Combine all ingredients except oil and pat mixture into eight small patties. Heat oil in a large skillet and fry patties about 20 minutes, turning, until brown and crisp on both sides.

Rick Graham
Kingsville

Easy Turkey Divan

1 10-ounce package frozen chopped broccoli
1 cup chopped cooked turkey
½ cup mayonnaise
1 can cream of chicken soup
1 cup uncooked Minute rice
2 tablespoons chopped onion
⅛ teaspoon poultry seasoning
¼ teaspoon garlic powder
½ teaspoon salt
¼ teaspoon pepper
¼ teaspoon paprika
2 tablespoons Pace mild picante sauce
½ to ¾ cup grated cheddar cheese

Cook broccoli and place in bottom of a 1-quart casserole dish. Layer turkey on top of broccoli. Mix together remaining ingredients except cheese and spread on top. Cover with cheese. Bake at 350 degrees for 30 minutes or until cheese bubbles. Serve with picante sauce. (This dish freezes well.)

Sharon Roden
Crandall

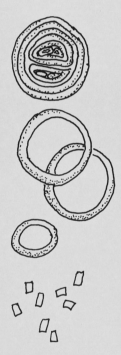

Rice Surprise

1 pound lean ground turkey
1 cup chopped onion
1 cup chopped bell pepper
1 tablespoon chili powder
1 tablespoon salt
1 teaspoon garlic
1 32-ounce can tomatoes
3 cups cooked rice
3 cups raw shredded cabbage
1 cup sour cream
8 ounces Monterey Jack cheese, shredded

Cook turkey, onion, and bell pepper until brown. Drain off any excess grease. Add chili powder, salt, garlic, tomatoes, rice, and cabbage. Bring to a boil, then lower heat and simmer 10 minutes. Add sour cream and stir. Top with cheese. Keep warm until cheese melts. Serves 10.

Wilma Schertz
Krum

Rice and Turkey Balls

1 cup uncooked Minute rice
1 pound ground turkey
1 egg, slightly beaten
2 teaspoons grated onion
2 teaspoons salt
⅛ teaspoon marjoram
dash of pepper
2 8-ounce cans tomato sauce mixed with ½ cup water
½ teaspoon sugar

Combine rice with turkey, egg, onion, salt, marjoram, pepper, and ½ cup tomato sauce. Mix lightly. Shape mixture into 18 balls and place in skillet. Add sugar to remaining 2 cups of tomato sauce. Pour over turkey balls in skillet. Bring mixture to a boil. Reduce heat and simmer covered for 15 minutes, basting occasionally. Makes 6 servings.

Mrs. R. W. Burns
Keller

Turkey Meat Loaf

2 pounds ground turkey
3 tablespoons diced green chilies
⅛ cup flour
½ onion, diced
1 egg
1 8-ounce can tomato sauce

Mix all ingredients together except tomato sauce and transfer to microwave pan. Pour tomato sauce over the loaf. Microwave on high for 8 to 10 minutes. Serve.

Vergene Vogel
El Paso

MEATS

Rector Story first began
making saddles in 1938
as an apprentice at Do-
naho Saddle Shop in
San Angelo. He now
owns the shop, which
was established in
1890.

BEEF

Oven-Barbecued Brisket à la San Angelo

1 5- or 6-pound brisket, trimmed
Worcestershire sauce
celery salt
onion salt
lemon pepper
garlic season-all
Liquid Smoke
teriyaki sauce
your favorite barbecue sauce

Sprinkle meat with seasonings to taste. Marinate in refrigerator overnight. Wrap tightly in foil and bake at 250 degrees for 5 hours. Remove foil, spread meat with barbecue sauce, and cook for 1 hour uncovered. Cool and slice. (This freezes well.)

Mr. and Mrs. Rector Story
San Angelo

Swiss Steak South Texas Style

2 pounds beef, diced
2 fresh tomatoes, chopped, or 1 can tomato paste
1 bell pepper, sliced
2 carrots, sliced
1 small onion, diced fine
cayenne pepper to taste
1 tablespoon salt
1 teaspoon pepper

Sauté beef and vegetables. Bake at 225 degrees for at least 12 hours. Great served with salad and potatoes. Serves 8.

Kent Lawrence
Zapata

Firehouse Smothered Steak

2½ pounds round steak
5 to 6 tablespoons oil or as needed
5 packages mushroom gravy mix
water
1 rounded tablespoon beef bouillon
2 medium onions, quartered
8 ounces fresh mushrooms, sliced

Trim meat and cut into 2-inch cubes. In a large skillet, brown meat slightly in hot oil. In a roasting pan combine gravy mix with water according to directions on package. Add bouillon and mix well. Add meat, onions, and mushrooms. Cover and bake at 325 degrees on top rack of oven for 3 hours. Check after about 2 hours to be sure meat is covered with gravy and is not sticking to pan. Add extra water and stir as needed. Serve with mashed potatoes, cole slaw, a large slice of raw onion, and cornbread. Serves 6 to 8 or 1 hungry firefighter!

Rodney Gant
Plano

Chicken-Fried Steak with Gravy

4 cube steaks (4 to 5 ounces each)
3 eggs, beaten
1 cup flour seasoned with 1 teaspoon pepper
1 to 2 cups vegetable oil
1 cup milk
salt and pepper to taste

Dip steaks in beaten eggs, then dredge in seasoned flour. Dip again in eggs, then in flour. In a heavy skillet heat oil to a depth of ½ inch until very hot but not smoking. Fry steaks in hot oil and cook 6 to 8 minutes or until golden brown. Turn and fry on other side 3 to 4 minutes. Remove with slotted spoon and drain on paper towels.

To make gravy, pour off all but 2 tablespoons of oil in skillet. Return to heat, and sprinkle 2 tablespoons seasoned flour over the hot oil, stirring constantly for a full minute, scraping up browned bits of crust from bottom of skillet. Add milk, a little at a time. Continue cooking and stirring until gravy is thick. Add salt and pepper.

Dolores R. Booher
Irving

Forgotten Roast

1 4- to 5-pound chuck roast
1 package dry onion soup mix

Sprinkle roast with onion soup. Place on aluminum foil. Fold edges, sealing well. Bake at 300 degrees for 3 hours.

Erlean Rutherford
Mesquite

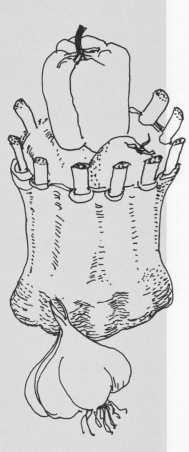

Mexicali Roast

1 2- to 3-pound crown roast
vegetable oil
1 medium green bell pepper, chopped
1 medium onion, chopped
2 large cloves garlic, minced
1 cup uncooked rice
1 can whole tomatoes
¾ cup water
1 package Chili-O mix

Brown roast in a small amount of oil; remove from pot. Brown bell pepper, onion, garlic, and rice. Return roast to pot. Pour tomatoes and rice over roast and vegetables and sprinkle with half the chili mix. Cover and cook over low heat for about 1½ hours.

Jo Ann Ware
Galveston

Pepper Steak

1½ pounds round steak
oil or butter
1 medium onion, cut into ¼-inch slices
2 medium bell peppers, cut into ¾-inch strips
1 cup beer
1 teaspoon garlic salt
1 teaspoon ginger
1 teaspoon salt and pepper
1 tablespoon cornstarch
2 tablespoons sugar
2 tablespoons soy sauce
2 medium tomatoes
hot cooked rice

Trim any excess fat from meat. Cut meat into strips about 2 inches by ¼ inch. Heat oil in a large skillet. Brown meat in oil for 5 minutes. Add onion and bell peppers. Stir in beer, garlic salt, ginger, salt, and pepper. Heat to boiling. Reduce heat, cover, and simmer approximately 15 minutes. Blend cornstarch, sugar, and soy sauce and stir into meat. Cook, stirring constantly, until mixture boils. Cut tomatoes into eighths and place on meat mixture. Cover and cook over low heat just until tomatoes are heated through. Serve over rice. Serves 4 to 5.

Mary Brown
Montgomery

Beef Burgundy with Rice

5 medium onions, sliced thin
2 tablespoons bacon drippings or shortening
2 pounds boneless beef chuck, cubed
2 tablespoons flour
salt
pepper
thyme
marjoram
½ cup beef bouillon
1 cup red wine
½ pound fresh mushrooms, sliced
4 cups cooked rice

In a heavy skillet, cook onions in bacon drippings until brown; remove onions from pan. Add beef and more drippings if necessary. Brown beef cubes well on all sides and sprinkle with flour and seasonings. Stir in bouillon and wine. Simmer very slowly for 2½ to 3 hours or until meat is tender. If necessary, add more bouillon and red wine (one part bouillon to two parts wine) to keep barely covered with liquid. Return onions to pan and add mushrooms; cook 30 minutes longer, adding liquid if necessary. Adjust seasonings to taste. Serve over rice.

Fran Barnhill
Hearne

Barbecue Meatballs

3 pounds ground chuck
1 13-ounce can evaporated milk
½ teaspoon salt
2 cups oatmeal
1 cup chopped onion
2 teaspoons chili powder
2 eggs or ½ cup Egg Beaters
½ teaspoon garlic powder
½ teaspoon black pepper
3 cups catsup
2 tablespoons Liquid Smoke
½ cup chopped onion
1 cup brown sugar, packed
½ teaspoon garlic powder

Combine meat, milk, salt, oatmeal, onion, chili powder, eggs, garlic powder, and pepper and mix well. Shape into walnut-size balls. Place in one layer in shallow pans. Mix remaining ingredients well and pour over meatballs. Bake 45 minutes at 350 degrees. This makes a large amount but freezes well.

Delphine F. Wilemon
Dallas

Barbecue Cups

2 cups buttermilk biscuit mix
½ cup cold water
1 pound ground beef
1 clove garlic, crushed
½ cup chopped onion
½ cup barbecue sauce
½ cup shredded cheddar cheese

Mix buttermilk biscuit mix and cold water to form soft dough. Beat vigorously with a spoon for 20 strokes. Drop by spoonfuls into 12 medium ungreased muffin cups. Press dough on bottom and up sides of each cup with floured hands. Stirring frequently, cook ground beef, garlic, and onion in a skillet until beef is brown; drain. Stir in barbecue sauce; heat through. Spoon beef mixture into cups; sprinkle with cheese. Bake at 400 degrees about 15 minutes or until crust is golden brown.

Janice Davis
Richardson

Beef Barbecue

1 pound round steak
½ stick butter or margarine
1 onion, chopped
2 tablespoons brown sugar
2 tablespoons vinegar
½ cup beef stock
1 8-ounce can tomato sauce
2 tablespoons Worcestershire sauce
1½ teaspoons salt
¼ teaspoon pepper
1 teaspoon prepared mustard

Place steak in pressure cooker with enough water to cover and cook about 30 minutes. Or place steak in a large pot with enough water to cover and cook 1 to 2 hours or until meat is tender and falls apart. Remove meat from pan and save stock. In a skillet sauté onion in butter until transparent. Add remaining ingredients. Simmer for 20 to 30 minutes or until sauce is thick. Shred cooked meat and add to sauce mixture. Serve on flour tortillas with toppings such as lettuce, tomato, cheese, and onion.

Denise McClaugherty
Cleburne

Tamale Pie

2 tablespoons vegetable oil
½ cup chopped bell pepper
⅓ cup chopped onion
1 clove garlic, chopped fine
1 pound ground round steak
1 14-ounce can peeled tomatoes, undrained
1 teaspoon ground coriander
½ cup chopped ripe olives
1½ tablespoons chili power
1 teaspoon salt
2 10½-ounce cans condensed beef broth
1½ cups water
1½ cans yellow cornmeal
1 tablespoon butter or margarine

When Cortes arrived in Mexico in 1519, the Aztec Indians served him "tamalli"— chopped venison in cornmeal wrapped in corn husks and steamed. Tamalli turned up later on the East Coast of North America where Captain John Smith found it being prepared by the Virginia Indians in 1612. Tamale pie is a modern version of the original.

In a skillet, heat oil and sauté bell pepper, onion, and garlic until soft but not brown. Add beef; brown well. Add tomatoes with their liquid, coriander, olives, chili powder, and salt. Mix well and cook over medium heat for 20 minutes. In a medium saucepan, heat broth to boiling. Combine water and cornmeal; gradually stir into boiling broth and cook until very thick. In a greased 12″ × 8″ × 2″ baking dish, line bottom and sides with half the cornmeal mush. Add meat mixture, then cover top with remaining mush. Cook slightly; dot with butter. Bake at 350 degrees for 45 minutes.

Dott and Marvin Bull
Celina

Mexican Egg Rolls

1 pound ground beef
1 package taco flavoring mix
¼ cup water
1 No. 2 can refried beans
2 cups shredded cheddar cheese
1 package egg roll wrappers (large size)

Brown beef, then add taco mix and water. Let simmer about 5 minutes. Cool. Fill each egg roll wrapper with 1 heaping tablespoon refried beans, 1 tablespoon meat mixture, and 1 tablespoon cheese. Moisten ends of wrapper with water, fold ends, and roll. Deep-fry until golden brown and serve with hot sauce. Serves 12.

Jo Ann Beal
San Antonio

Nonspicy, Hearty Chili

2 pounds ground round
3 to 4 large yellow onions, chopped
2 small cans tomato paste
2 cans red kidney beans, drained

Brown meat in a frying pan, stirring to make it crumbly. Add chopped onions and stir for a few minutes. Then add beans and tomato paste. Stir well until all ingredients are mixed well. Cover and simmer 1 hour. Serve with soda crackers.

Peggy Snyder
Comfort

This chili is excellent for children. I raised three of them in the Northern Wisconsin winters on this, and there's nothing better.

Green Enchiladas

2 pounds ground meat
salt and pepper to taste
2 cups milk
½ pound Velveeta cheese
pinch of salt
20 to 30 tortillas
5 tablespoons salad oil
½ cup chopped onion
2 cups grated cheddar cheese
1 4-ounce can green chilies
1 2-ounce jar chopped pimientos

Brown meat and season with salt and pepper. In a saucepan combine milk, Velveeta cheese, and salt and heat very slowly until cheese is melted. Dip each tortilla in hot oil until limp. Drain. On each tortilla place some meat, onion, and cheddar cheese. Roll up and place in a 9″ × 13″ baking dish. Top with milk mixture, green chilies, and pimientos. Cover with foil and bake at 350 degrees for 40 minutes.

Matthew Kast
Fredericksburg

Mexican Casserole

2 pounds ground meat
1 large onion
1 can cream of mushroom soup
1 can cream of chicken soup
1 small can green chilies, chopped and drained
1 small can evaporated milk
1 can enchilada sauce
1 pound Velveeta cheese, sliced
1 large bag Doritos or tortillas

Sauté meat and onion until meat is almost done. Add remaining ingredients except cheese and Doritos. Mix well. Line a casserole dish with Doritos and pour half the meat mixture over them. Top with Doritos and the cheese. Add remaining meat mixture, Doritos, and cheese. Bake at 300 degrees until cheese is melted. Do not add salt.

Peggy Moore
Mexia

I am 94 years old. If my dad, Allen Hailey, could get to town to get a bowl of chili and talk politics, he was very happy! He was born in Texas and was a cowboy when younger.

Mexican Meat with Cornbread Topping

1 pound ground beef
1 tablespoon cooking oil
2 cups cooked rice
1 16-ounce can tomatoes, undrained
1 teaspoon salt
⅛ teaspoon pepper
¼ to ½ teaspoon chili powder
4 tablespoons grated onion
1 cup cornbread mix

Cook meat in oil until browned. Add rice, tomatoes, salt, pepper, chili powder, and onion. Mix well, breaking tomatoes and meat into small pieces. Cook until thoroughly heated and liquid is absorbed. Prepare cornbread mix according to directions on package and pour batter over meat mixture. Bake at 425 degrees for 25 minutes or until cornbread is done. Add a small amount of water to meat mixture before baking if necessary. Serves 6.

Doris Sutton
Whitesboro

Pearlie Black's Cafe Chili

3 pounds dried pinto beans
salt to taste
3 pounds ground beef
1 large onion, chopped
1 level tablespoon minced garlic or 1 scant tablespoon garlic
    powder
3 8-ounce cans tomato paste
1½ cups sugar
½ cup vinegar
2 packages of William's chili powder
cayenne pepper to taste

Cook beans in an open kettle 40 minutes. Add salt and cook in a pressure cooker at 15 pounds of pressure for 45 minutes. In a large greased skillet brown ground beef. Add onion and garlic and simmer 15 minutes over low heat, stirring occasionally. Add tomato paste. Add beef mixture to beans and taste to correct seasoning. Add sugar, vinegar, chili powder, and cayenne pepper. Stir and simmer 10 minutes.

Ruth Hailey Stumpff
Amarillo

Top of Texas Chili

6 pounds lean coarse-ground chuck
2 large onions, diced
6 green chile peppers, diced
 (or 2 large bell peppers, diced)
5 dashes Tabasco sauce
10 dashes liquid garlic
2 teaspoons oregano
2 teaspoons black pepper
2 teaspoons cumin
12 ounces chili powder
6 teaspoons salt
12 teaspoons Kitchen Bouquet
4 16-ounce cans tomato sauce
4 16-ounce cans stewed tomatoes
1 5-ounce can diced hot chilies
1 to 3 teaspoons flour for thickening
water for thinning

Brown ground chuck in oil over high heat. Add onions and chile peppers and sauté with meat. Add Tabasco sauce, liquid garlic, oregano, black pepper, cumin, chili powder, salt, Kitchen Bouquet, tomato sauce, stewed tomatoes, and hot chilies and simmer for at least 2 hours. Taste to correct seasonings and add flour (to thicken) or water (to thin) if necessary. Simmer for approximately 1 more hour.

Pat Seagraves
Dalhart

Wendy's Killer Chili

2 pounds ground meat
2 large onions, chopped
1 32-ounce can tomato puree
1 can chopped green chilies
2 teaspoons salt
garlic salt to taste
5 tablespoons cayenne pepper
½ cup chili powder
3 tablespoons molasses
½ cup ground cumin
1 32-ounce can refried beans
2 cans kidney beans

I made this recipe up when I wanted to get my revenge on a Northerner who claimed there was no such thing as spicy Texas food. But the joke was on me because it was a hit!

Cook meat and sauté onions. Add puree and remaining ingredients except beans. Then add refried beans and kidney beans. Taste to correct seasonings. Cook a little bit more and let sit for a while. Reheat and serve.

Wendy Allen
Dublin

Remember that there are no tomatoes in real Texas chili. That deep red color comes from the chile peppers.

Bob's Bitchin' Chili

12 dried chile peppers (ancho, arbol, or japon variety) or to taste
1 teaspoon crushed pequin peppers or to taste
1 package Wick Fowler's 2-Alarm chili seasonings
4 pounds lean beef (or turkey), ground or cubed
1 cup dry red wine
5 fresh whole jalapeño peppers
2 to 3 cups water

Remove stems and seeds from dried chile peppers. Place in a small saucepan and add enough water to cover. Boil 10 to 15 minutes. Reserve liquid; transfer peppers to a blender or food processor. Process to form a thick paste, adding enough reserved liquid for processing (or use plain water for a milder chili). Add all chili seasonings except masa trigo. Lightly brown meat in a Dutch oven. Add paste and enough water to barely cover the meat (or use reserved liquid from boiling chilies for a hotter chili). Cook for 30 minutes, then add wine. Cook for 30 minutes and add jalapeños. Cook an additional 30 minutes and add masa trigo. Serve with cornbread.

Bob Phillips
Dallas

Wolf-at-the-Door Stew

1 pound lean ground beef
1 onion, chopped
1 can tomatoes, chopped
1 can green chilies, chopped
2 cans pinto beans

This stew was very popular during the Great Depression of the 1930s.

Brown the beef and add onion, tomatoes, and green chilies. Cook for 30 minutes. Add pinto beans and heat. Serve with warm flour or corn tortillas.

Kassy Maxwell
San Angelo

Gypsy Stew

1 pound ground beef
1 onion, chopped
1 bell pepper, chopped
2 cloves garlic, minced
1 medium bunch of celery, cut into bite-size pieces
1 tablespoon chili powder
¼ teaspoon cayenne pepper
salt and pepper to taste
1 16-ounce can tomatoes, undrained and chopped

Sauté ground beef, onion, bell pepper, and garlic. Add celery, chili powder, salt and pepper, and chopped tomatoes with juice. Simmer 35 minutes. Serve over mashed potatoes.

Margaret Olson
Watauga

This recipe is my own, and I have made it for fifty years. It has always been one of the family favorites.

Cowboy Stew

1 tablespoon margarine
1 pound ground meat
1 large onion, chopped
¼ cup chopped celery
¼ cup chopped bell pepper
1 clove garlic
¼ teaspoon sugar or more
3 or 4 carrots, sliced
1 can tomatoes
1 16-ounce can whole-kernel or cream-style corn
1 32-ounce can ranch-style beans
6 medium potatoes
3 cups water or more
salt and pepper to taste

Brown meat in margarine. Transfer to a large pot and add remaining ingredients. Cook until potatoes and carrots are done.

Marie Nash
Leona

This recipe makes a large amount and is good on a cold day or a busy one. Make a pan of cornbread and you have a full meal. This is also good to take to someone sick.

Tracy Sue's Stew for Two (or More!)

1 cup flour
1 teaspoon salt
1½ teaspoons pepper or to taste
1 pound stewmeat, cut into 1-inch cubes
½ cup chopped onion
½ cup chopped bell pepper
3 stalks celery, chopped
2 tablespoons cooking oil
1 can tomato soup
1 can water
½ cup dry red wine
4 small potatoes, cubed
4 carrots, sliced

Mix flour with salt and pepper. Coat stewmeat with seasoned flour. Brown onion, bell pepper, and celery in cooking oil (or use cooking spray to save calories). Mix tomato soup with water, pour over meat, mix well, and bake at 375 degrees for 1 hour. Add wine, potatoes, and carrots and bake 1 to 1½ hours or until potatoes are tender.

Tracy Phillips
Dallas

Texas Cowboy (Son-of-a-Gun) Stew

2 pounds beef heart
1 calf tongue
2 pounds beef honeycomb tripe
2 pounds calf sweetbreads
2 pounds liver
2 pounds calf brains
2 No. 2 cans hominy
2 No. 2 cans garbanzo beans
4 pounds potatoes, peeled and cut into 2-inch cubes
1 8-ounce can tomato sauce
1 teaspoon ground cumin
1 tablespoon cayenne pepper
salt and pepper to taste
6 medium onions, quartered
4 cloves garlic, mashed

ROUX
1 cup margarine
1 cup flour

Remove fat from heart. Boil heart, tongue, and tripe for 2 hours. Remove from water and let cool. Put sweetbreads, liver, and brains into same water and boil 15 minutes. Remove and let cool. Reserve broth. Remove all bone and gristle from heart and tongue and skin tongue. Cut into strips about 1 inch by ¼ inch. Cut tripe into ½-inch cubes. Skin liver and cut into ½-inch cubes. Remove skin, membrane, and tubes from sweetbreads and brains. Cut into bite-size pieces. Combine all prepared meat and remaining stew ingredients in a large pot or kettle. Add 3 quarts of the reserved broth (add water to make total amount if needed). Bring to a boil, lower heat, and simmer 2 hours. To make roux, melt margarine and add flour. Stir constantly and cook until flour becomes chocolate brown. Add to stew during last 10 minutes of cooking. Serve with cornbread, crackers, or biscuits. Serves 15 hungry cowboys or 30 average people.

Roaul L. Begley
Arlington

Mushroom Spaghetti

1½ pounds ground meat
1 small onion, chopped fine
salt and pepper to taste
1 tablespoon each of tarragon, oregano, and Italian seasoning
1 tablespoon garlic powder (or 1 clove fresh garlic)
2 cans Campbell's Golden Mushroom soup, undiluted
½ soup can of water
1 teaspoon Worcestershire sauce (optional)
1 large can sliced mushrooms

Crumble ground meat in a large skillet; brown meat and onion together. Add salt and pepper and other seasonings, then add soup and water. Simmer 30 minutes, uncovered; add Worcestershire sauce and mushrooms and heat through. Serve over spaghetti. Serves 4.

Jack Lyons
Dallas

In an effort to bring home cooking to an institutional setting, Kerr Dormitory at the University of North Texas in Denton placed this dish on its cafeteria menu. A computer was used to convert this recipe for four into a recipe that serves as many as 350.

I received this recipe from my mother, Mary Sykora. I have no idea where she came up with the recipe. This is excellent spaghetti if you like your spaghetti spicy.

Irish Italian Spaghetti

1 onion, chopped
2 tablespoons salad oil
1 pound lean ground beef
1 teaspoon salt
½ teaspoon black pepper
dash of cayenne pepper
½ teaspoon chili powder
½ teaspoon Tabasco sauce
1 teaspoon oregano
1 can cream of mushroom soup
1 can tomato soup
½ to 1 cup red cooking wine

Brown onion in hot oil; add meat and seasonings. Brown lightly; cover and simmer for 10 minutes. Drain off excess oil. Add soups and cooking wine; cover and simmer 45 minutes. Serve over cooked spaghetti.

Bob Sykora
Dallas

Western-Style Spaghetti

1 cup chopped onion
1½ cloves garlic, minced
1 bell pepper, chopped
4 tablespoons oil or drippings
1½ pounds ground meat
1½ cans tomato sauce
2 cups water
3 tablespoons Worcestershire sauce
¼ teaspoon pepper
1 teaspoon salt
1 10-ounce package spaghetti, cooked
2 cups grated sharp cheddar cheese

Lightly brown onion, garlic, and bell pepper in hot oil. Add meat, stirring until it is no longer pink. Add tomato sauce, water, and seasonings. Simmer 40 minutes. Place cooked spaghetti in casserole dish, cover with meat mixture, then top with cheese. Bake at 350 degrees until cheese melts.

Winifred Darsey
Matador

Pat's Lasagna

½ cup chopped onion
½ cup chopped bell pepper
3 tablespoons olive oil
1 pound extra lean ground round
2 cloves garlic
1½ cups water
3 6-ounce cans tomato paste
1 teaspoon Italian seasoning
½ teaspoon chili powder
salt to taste
¼ teaspoon black pepper
1 cup Romano cheese, grated
1 pound mozzarella cheese, grated
1 pound small-curd cottage cheese
12 ounces lasagna noodles

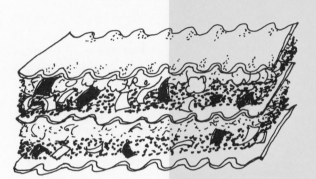

Sauté onion and bell pepper in olive oil in a large pan until limp. Add meat, separate well, and cook until meat is no longer pink. Mash garlic with a small amount of salt and add to meat. Add water, tomato paste, Italian seasoning, chili powder, salt, and pepper. Mix well and simmer over low heat for 30 minutes. (Sauce will be very thick.) Meanwhile cook noodles. In two 9″ × 13″ × 2″ baking pans, spread thin layer of sauce. Add layer of noodles and layer of each of the three cheeses. Repeat the noodles and cheese layers until all is used up. Sprinkle with Romano. Bake uncovered at 350 degrees for 45 minutes.

Pat McCauley
Del Rio

Crockpot Beans

1 onion, chopped
1 bell pepper, chopped
1 pound ground beef
1 can ranch-style beans
1 can tomato sauce
1 can water
1 teaspoon chili powder
salt and pepper

Brown ground meat with onion and bell pepper. Mix in remaining ingredients and transfer to a crockpot. Simmer several hours and serve over rice.

Mark Dubois
Nederland

My mother raised me on this. I remember one of my birthdays when Mom and Dad said, "Where do you want to go to eat?" My reply was that I wanted to eat at home and have Peas and Bread, salad, and pineapple upside-down cake.

Beef Tenderloin Elegante

4 beef tenderloin steaks (½ inch thick)
1 tablespoon margarine or butter
4 tablespoons brandy, divided
½ cup sour cream
2 tablespoons catsup
¼ teaspoon salt
2 dashes of Worcestershire sauce
2 drops of hot pepper sauce
pinch of ground thyme

In a skillet, brown steaks in butter on both sides to desired doneness. Remove from heat and spoon 2 tablespoons brandy over steaks. Place steaks on warm platter and keep hot. Combine remaining brandy, sour cream, catsup, and remaining ingredients. Add to skillet, stirring until hot. Spoon sauce over steaks.

Sarah L. Helford
Dallas

Peas and Bread

½ teaspoon baking soda
1 cup buttermilk
1 cup cornmeal
½ cup flour
1 teaspoon salt
2 eggs
½ cup oil
1 onion, chopped
1 can black-eyed peas, drained slightly
1 can green chilies
1 small can cream-style corn
1 pound ground meat, browned with onions and drained
½ to 1 pound cheddar cheese, grated

Add soda to buttermilk and set aside. Mix cornmeal, flour, salt, eggs, oil, and buttermilk. Add peas, green chilies, corn, meat, and all the grated cheese except a small amount for the top. Stir to mix and pour into a large well-greased skillet or 9" × 13" pan. Top with remaining cheese. Bake at 350 degrees for 45 minutes. Serve with picante sauce.

Jeff Cantrell
Sherman

Bob Mohel's Stuffed Bell Peppers

8 bell peppers
1 to 1½ pounds lean ground round
1 small onion, chopped
1 small cooked potato, cubed
4 tablespoons frozen peas
4 tablespoons frozen corn
8 slices American cheese, cut into ¼-inch pieces
1 4-ounce jar pimientos
8 saltine crackers
8 serrano peppers (optional)
¼ teaspoon fresh-ground black pepper
¼ teaspoon celery salt
¼ teaspoon Mrs. Dash's table blend
¼ teaspoon flavor enhancer
¼ teaspoon garlic
¼ teaspoon spicy Season-All
¼ teaspoon creole seasoning
8 teaspoons butter

Core peppers, remove seeds, boil until tender, drain, and set aside. Sauté ground meat and onion; add potato, peas, and corn and cook until heated through. Transfer to a large bowl and add remaining ingredients except butter; mix well. Stuff peppers and top with 1 teaspoon butter. Bake at 300 degrees until butter melts. Serve hot.

Bob Mohel
San Antonio

Stuff

2 pounds ground round
2 teaspoons Lawrey's seasoned salt
2 teaspoons Lawrey's seasoned pepper
1 teaspoon dried onion flakes (or 2 teaspoons chopped onion)
1 8-ounce can whole-kernel corn, drained
1 16-ounce can ranch-style beans
1 8-ounce can Ro-tel tomatoes, blended in blender
½ to ¾ pound Kraft American cheese, grated

Combine ground round with salt, pepper, and onion. Cook until brown. Add corn, beans, and tomatoes. Cook until heated through. Add cheese, stirring until melted. Simmer, covered, approximately 15 minutes. Serve hot with cornbread and a salad.

Karen J. Hayter
Arlington

When my husband and I were married twenty-one years ago, we had almost no money. At the end of a particularly difficult month, we were looking for something to have for dinner. We combined everything left over in the pantry and came up with Stuff. It has been a family tradition and favorite at the end of every month since that time.

This meat loaf recipe has been passed down to the women in my family for many, many years. When I first fixed this for my boyfriend, he said that it was the best meat loaf he had ever eaten. After thirteen years of marriage he still says it is the best.

Aunt Ann's Meat Loaf

1 pound ground beef
2 eggs, slightly beaten
¾ cup milk
2 slices bread, torn into pieces (or 6 crackers, broken into
  pieces)
1 teaspoon salt
½ onion, chopped
½ teaspoon sage
¼ teaspoon black pepper
4 slices of bacon

PIQUANT SAUCE
¼ cup catsup
3 tablespoons brown sugar
1 teaspoon dry mustard
¼ teaspoon nutmeg

Combine ground meat, eggs, milk, and bread and mix well. Then add salt, onion, sage, and pepper. To make Piquant Sauce, in a separate bowl mix together catsup, brown sugar, dry mustard, and nutmeg. Add half the sauce to the meat mixture and mix well. Transfer to a baking dish and spread remaining sauce evenly over the top. Cover with bacon slices. Bake at 350 degrees for 1 hour.

Vicki Hill Ramsey
Gun Barrel City

Cabbage Rolls

2 pounds lean ground beef
2 teaspoons salt
½ teaspoon pepper
1 tablespoon chili powder
1 cup cooked rice
1 small onion, grated
3 8-ounce cans tomato sauce
12 large cabbage leaves
¼ cup brown sugar
¼ cup lemon juice
1 tablespoon Worcestershire sauce

Cook ground meat until it changes color. Drain off fat and cool. Add salt, pepper, chili powder, rice, onion, and 1 can tomato sauce. Blanch cabbage leaves in boiling water for 4 or 5 minutes; drain. Place equal portions of meat mixture in the center of each cabbage leaf. Roll up and secure with a toothpick. Place rolls in roaster. Mix remaining tomato sauce, Worcestershire sauce, brown sugar, and lemon juice and pour over cabbage rolls. Cover roaster and bake at 350 degrees for 40 to 50 minutes. Baste with the sauce.

Norma Hayter
Lefors

Doc Evans's Six Flags Over Texas Bunburgers

⅓ pound ground chuck (U.S. Choice)
1 slice American cheese
1 slice Spanish onion
2 slices Kosher or Polish dill pickle
1 slice Confederate (hickory-smoked) bacon
1 teaspoon Mexican mole sauce
1 teaspoon French Dijon mustard
1 Daughters of the Republic of Texas Bun, sliced

DAUGHTERS OF THE REPUBLIC OF TEXAS BUNS
1 cup lukewarm water
2 teaspoons sugar
1 envelope dry yeast
3 cups sifted flour
1½ teaspoons salt

Grill meat patty to medium rare. Grill onion slice to medium soft. Spread grilled patty with mole and mustard, then top with onion, pickle, bacon, cheese, and top half of bun. Grill until cheese melts, then stack onto grilled or toasted bottom half of bun. Serve hot. Serves 1. To make Daughters of the Republic of Texas Buns, place water in mixing bowl and add sugar and dry yeast. Stir until dissolved. Add 1½ cups flour and salt and beat hard with a spoon (about 2 minutes). Gradually add 1¼ to 1½ cups flour, mixing first with a spoon, then with hands to make a smooth springy ball of dough (about 5 minutes). Cover with a towel and place in a warm place about 25 minutes or until doubled. Divide dough into four or six pieces and flatten on a well-oiled board with oiled hands. Place each in a muffin ring for small buns or make a large bun ring from heavy aluminum foil for four buns. Cover; let rise in warm place 25 minutes or until doubled. Bake at 400 degrees for 20 minutes or until golden brown. Turn out onto rack and slice when cool.

Dr. Keith R. Evans
Dallas

This recipe, winner of a hamburger cook-off in Dallas, represents the governments that have ruled Texas.

Saucy Beef

½ pound ground beef
1 large onion, chopped
1 clove garlic, chopped
½ pound German sausage, sliced
1 16-ounce can sauerkraut
1 16-ounce can chopped tomatoes
1 4-ounce can chopped green chilies
½ teaspoon caraway seeds
1 bay leaf
½ teaspoon salt
½ teaspoon pepper

Sauté ground beef until no longer pink. Transfer to a large casserole dish. Sauté onion and garlic until onion is clear. Add to casserole with remaining ingredients, mixing well. Bake at 350 degrees for 1 hour.

Adeline S. Gauthier
Columbus, New Mexico

Pinto Beef Casserole

1 pound ground beef
½ cup chopped onion
½ cup chopped bell pepper
1 clove garlic, minced
1 15-ounce can tomato sauce
2 teaspoons chili powder
1 teaspoon salt
3 cups hot cooked rice
1 can pinto beans, drained
1 cup shredded Velveeta cheese

Brown ground beef in a skillet. Add onion, bell pepper, and garlic and cook until tender. Add tomato sauce, chili powder, and salt, mixing well. Grease a 2-quart baking dish. Arrange meat mixture, rice, beans, and ¾ cup cheese in layers, beginning and ending with the meat mixture. Sprinkle remaining ¼ cup cheese on top. Bake at 350 degrees for 20 minutes or until bubbly. Serves 6.

Mrs. Travis H. Tate
San Marcos

Greek Meatballs with Gravy

1 pound ground meat
salt and pepper to taste
½ medium onion, chopped fine
1 teaspoon minced mint leaves (optional)
1 tablespoon parsley flakes
1 egg
2 tablespoons uncooked rice
1 cup beef stock
1 cup water

GRAVY
2 tablespoons grated onion
vegetable shortening
3 tablespoons flour
4 to 5 cups water
4 to 5 beef bouillon cubes
pepper to taste
dash of cayenne pepper
½ cup heavy cream

Combine meat, salt, pepper, onion, mint, parsley, egg, and rice. Mix well and form into walnut-sized balls. Heat stock and water to boiling. Drop in meatballs. Heat to boiling, then reduce heat and simmer for 45 minutes. Transfer to a warm plate. To make gravy, sauté onion in shortening until clear. Add flour and brown slightly. Add water and beef bouillon cubes. Simmer until smooth. Season with pepper and a dash of cayenne, then add cream. Add the cooked meatballs, cover, and simmer over very low heat for 20 minutes. Keep warm in a chafing dish. Serve alone or over cooked rice or noodles.

John Keen
Clifton

This year in my sixth-grade social studies class, when we had to do a project on Greece, we had the choice of cooking a Greek dish. I got one of my mom's cookbooks and she helped me find this recipe for Greek meatballs. My class and my teacher thought they were delicious!

Gwen's Okra Skillet

4 slices of bacon
1 16-ounce package frozen okra
1 medium onion, diced
1 pound ground beef
1 cup rice, cooked
1 16-ounce can tomatoes
1 8-ounce can tomato sauce
1 teaspoon sugar
salt and pepper to taste
pinch of chili powder

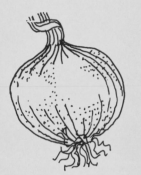

In a large skillet, fry bacon until crisp. Drain on paper towels, crumble, and set aside. Fry okra and onion in bacon grease until browned. In a separate pan, brown ground meat and drain off grease. Add meat, bacon, and remaining ingredients to okra and onion mixture, mixing well. Simmer until heated through. Serves 4 to 6.

Gwen Brown
Decatur

Quick Casserole

1 pound ground beef
1 small onion, chopped
1 package macaroni and cheese mix
1 17-ounce can whole-kernel corn, drained
2 8-ounce cans tomato sauce
salt and pepper to taste
1 cup Velveeta cheese or more

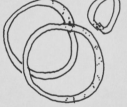

In a skillet, cook ground beef and onion until lightly browned. Drain off grease. Meanwhile prepare macaroni and cheese according to the instructions on the package. Transfer ground beef mixture and macaroni and cheese to a 2-quart casserole dish. Add corn and tomato sauce and mix well. Top with cheese. Bake covered at 350 degrees for 30 minutes or until bubbly. Serves 4 or more.

Teresa Iraggi
Victoria

Santa Fe Fiesta

1 pound lean ground beef
salt and pepper to taste
garlic powder to taste
2 teaspoons chili powder
2 cups hot water
1 cup mild salsa
1 package Sour Cream and Scallions Noodle-Roni
1 14½-ounce can Del Monte Original stewed tomatoes, drained
8 ounces Monterey Jack or colby cheese, grated

Brown beef in a skillet and add salt, pepper, garlic powder, chili powder, water, and salsa. Bring to a boil. Stir in noodle mix. Simmer over medium heat for 6 to 8 minutes or until most of the liquid is absorbed. Stir occasionally. Sprinkle tomatoes and cheese over mixture. Turn off heat. Cover. Let stand until cheese melts. Serves 6.

Colette Wiley
Mansfield

Mac-La-Dell

1 cup uncooked elbow macaroni
¼ cup fine-chopped yellow onion
½ cup fine-chopped celery
½ to ¾ pound lean ground beef
1 can cream of mushroom soup
½ cup canned tomatoes
½ cup cubed mild cheddar cheese
3 tablespoons milk

Cook macaroni according to instructions on package and drain. Sauté onion and celery in a saucepan; add beef, cook until brown, and drain off excess grease. Transfer to a 3-quart saucepan and add remaining ingredients. Cook uncovered over low heat, stirring occasionally, until cheese is melted.

Dell Fitzgibbon
Grand Prairie

Real Texas Menudo

4 pounds beef tripe
4 quarts beef broth (or 3 quarts beef broth and 1 quart tomato juice)
1 head of garlic
1½ pounds stewmeat
2½ tablespoons salt
1 heaping tablespoon black peppercorns
2 bay leaves
1 or 2 teaspoons cumin or to taste
1 teaspoon oregano
3 heaping tablespoons chili powder or to taste
1 small can green chilies (plabonoes preferred), undrained
2 cans yellow or white hominy, drained
2 cups coarse-chopped onions
1 cup coarse-chopped fresh cilantro
lemon wedges

I got this recipe from a camp cook called Yeller Dog, who was preparing the menudo in a cast-iron pot under a live oak tree near Bandera during a spring thunderstorm. He wouldn't leave the menudo pot to take shelter from the weather. I stayed with him by the campfire, getting drenched while making notes on the back of a handbill.

Place tripe in cold water to cover, bring to a rolling boil, and boil for 15 minutes. Discard water and scrape off most of the fat and membrane from the tripe. Cut tripe into 2-inch squares, return to pot, and add beef broth. Puncture each garlic clove with a sharp knife, wrap entire head in cheesecloth, and add to broth along with meat, salt, peppercorns, bay leaves, cumin, oregano, chili powder, and green chilies. Bring to a boil and simmer about 2 hours or until tripe can be easily cut with a fork. Skim off any fat that comes to the surface. During last 30 minutes of cooking, correct seasonings. Remove and discard garlic and add hominy during final 10 minutes of cooking. Mix onions and cilantro in a bowl. Ladle menudo into individual serving bowls. Garnish with onions and cilantro and add a squeeze of lemon juice to taste.

David K. Winston
Houston

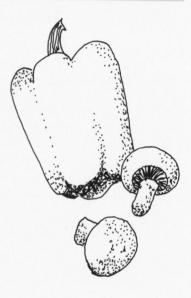

Veal Scallopini

1½ teaspoons salt
1½ teaspoons paprika
¾ cup olive oil
¼ cup lemon juice
1 to 2 cloves garlic, split
1 teaspoon prepared mustard
¼ teaspoon nutmeg
¾ teaspoon sugar
1½ to 2 pounds veal, sliced thin
¼ cup flour
¼ cup olive oil or shortening
1 medium onion, sliced thin
1 bell pepper, julienned
1 to 1½ cups chicken bouillon
¼ pound mushrooms
1 tablespoon butter
12 pimiento-stuffed olives
2 tablespoons dry sherry

In 1961, while stationed in Massachusetts, my wife and I discovered this recipe in a two-bit paperback cookbook that we have long since lost. It has been my traditional birthday dinner ever since.

Combine first eight ingredients, mix well, pour over the veal, and let stand for 15 to 30 minutes. Remove garlic slivers and reserve sauce. Dredge veal in flour and brown in a skillet with olive oil. Place in a 9″ × 13″ casserole dish. Spread the onion and bell pepper on top of veal. Combine chicken bouillon with the reserved sauce and pour over veal. Bake at 350 degrees for 35 or 40 minutes. Meanwhile clean and sauté mushrooms in butter; slice olives about ¹⁄₁₆ inch thick. When veal is done, sprinkle with mushrooms, olives, and sherry and cook for about 5 more minutes. Serve with creamed potatoes, steamed broccoli, asparagus, or steamed or glazed carrots. Serves 4.

Ira Sterling, Jr.
Universal City

Picnic Salami

4 pounds ground beef (maximum fat content 25%)
3 tablespoons Morton's curing salt
2 tablespoons Liquid Smoke
1½ teaspoons garlic powder
1½ teaspoons ground pepper (or 1½ teaspoons whole black
    peppercorns)

Place all ingredients in a large bowl and mix well. Cover tightly and chill for 24 hours. Divide mixture into fourths. Shape each fourth into a compact 8-inch log and place each log on a 12″ × 18″ piece of cheap white nylon net. Roll up tightly. Tie ends with string. Place logs on a rack in a broiler pan and bake at 225 degrees for 4 hours. Turn after the first 2 hours and before the last 30 minutes. Remove from oven and discard net. Pat rolls well with paper towels to absorb excess fat. Cool slightly, then wrap in foil. Refrigerate or freeze. Makes 3 pounds. Keeps in refrigerator for three weeks, in freezer for three months.

Frances H. and John M. Johnson
Cameron

We've been enjoying this for over ten years.

John M. Johnson has built a scale model of his Central Texas hometown of Cameron.

LAMB

Leg of Lamb

1 5- to 6-pound unboned leg of lamb
3 cloves fresh garlic, cut into slivers
4 strips of bacon
salt to taste
fresh-ground pepper to taste
veal or beef stock or bouillon

This is great for Sunday dinner—you can put it in the oven and forget it!

Trim and clean leg of lamb. Pierce in several places and insert garlic slivers. Cover with raw bacon strips and refrigerate, covered, overnight. Allow lamb to return to room temperature. Place in roasting pan and fill to ½ inch of top with stock or bouillon. Cover and bake at 325 degrees for 2 hours. Remove bacon strips and bake for 1½ to 2 hours more. Uncover during last 30 minutes to allow lamb to brown. When golden brown and fork tender, remove from oven; drain and use liquid for brown gravy if desired. Serve with browned new potatoes and a tossed green salad.

Valerie Tucker
Argyle

PORK

"TNT" Grilled Barbecued Ribs

4 to 6 pounds large pork ribs
1 medium onion, sliced
1 tablespoon ground cinnamon
1 tablespoon sweet basil
1½ teaspoons allspice
1½ teaspoons ginger
1½ teaspoons seasoned salt
1 teaspoon red pepper
3 whole bay leaves
2 cloves garlic, crushed
water
2 cups barbecue sauce
½ cup honey
1 tablespoon hot sauce

Place ribs in large pot. Combine next nine ingredients with enough water to cover ribs. Boil 30 to 45 minutes or until tender. Remove ribs from pot and place on grill, meat side down. Grill until browned. Mix barbecue sauce, honey, and hot sauce. Turn ribs and baste with sauce mixture. Grill 10 to 15 minutes more.

Arthur Thompson
Plano

Special Barbecued Ribs

1 tablespoon celery seed
1 tablespoon chili powder
¼ cup brown sugar
1 tablespoon salt
1 teaspoon paprika
2½ pounds spareribs
1 8-ounce can tomato sauce
¼ cup vinegar

Combine celery seed, chili powder, sugar, salt, and paprika. Rub one-third of mixture on ribs. To remaining mixture add tomato sauce and vinegar; heat. Cook ribs over low heat until tender, basting frequently with sauce.

Aleathia Renee Parrish
Killeen

Spareribs with Caraway Kraut

3 pounds spareribs, cut into serving pieces
2 teaspoons salt
¼ teaspoon pepper
1 No. 2½ can sauerkraut (about 3½ cups), undrained
2 medium carrots, sliced
1 tart unpeeled apple, chopped fine
1½ cups tomato juice
2 tablespoons brown sugar
3 teaspoons caraway seed

Season ribs with salt and pepper; place in Dutch oven. Combine kraut, including liquid, with remaining ingredients and spoon over ribs. Bake covered at 350 degrees 2½ to 3 hours or until done, basting several times with kraut mixture during last hour of cooking. Serve ribs with kraut and pot juices.

Gen Hullums
Freer

Carne Asada

1 tablespoon chili powder
1 teaspoon cumin
1 teaspoon paprika
1 teaspoon oregano
1 teaspoon sugar
1 beef bouillon cube mixed with ½ cup water
1 onion, sliced
2 pork chops, diced
1 pound sirloin, diced
½ teaspoon garlic salt
1 cup water
1 teaspoon flour mixed with ½ cup water

Mix all ingredients. Cook 2½ hours over low heat. Serve over rice.

J. T. Embrey
San Antonio

Green Chili Stew

1 cup dried pinto beans
2 quarts water
1½ pounds lean boneless pork roast, trimmed and diced into ½-inch cubes
2 tablespoons cooking oil
2 large onions, chopped fine
1 pound white potatoes, peeled and diced into ½-inch cubes
16 ounces chicken broth
16 ounces canned tomatoes
¼ teaspoon ground oregano
¼ teaspoon minced garlic
1 tablespoon ground cumin
8 ounces chopped green chilies or to taste
cayenne pepper to taste

Wash pinto beans and soak in water overnight. Cook until tender. In a large kettle heat oil and sauté onions until clear. Add pork cubes, toss with onions, and cook until pork is lightly browned. Add potatoes, chicken broth, tomatoes, oregano, garlic, cumin, and green chilies. Drain and rinse pinto beans. Add to stew, cover, reduce heat, and simmer 1 to 2 hours or until potatoes are tender. Add water if necessary during cooking. Add cayenne pepper. Serve with cornbread or sopapillas and honey.

Ira Gasser
Garland

Scouter's Survival Stew

2 28-ounce cans tomatoes
1 10-ounce can Ro-tel tomatoes and green chilies
1 pound smoked sausage
1 pound carrots, sliced
half to whole bunch of celery, sliced
1 pound onions, chopped
potatoes, peeled and cut into bite-size pieces, or pearled barley,
    cooked and drained (optional)

In an 8- to 10-quart stewpot, heat tomatoes and tomatoes and
green chilies over low heat, breaking up into pieces with a spoon.
Slice sausage lengthwise and cut into bite-size pieces. Add carrots, celery, onions, and potatoes (if using barley, add just before
serving). Bring to a boil, cover, reduce heat, and simmer at least
1 hour or more if needed. Serves 6 to 10.

Clint Lanier
Tyler

Country Stew

2 tablespoons butter
2 tablespoons oil
1 large onion, chopped
6 carrots, cut into pieces
2 stalks celery, cut into pieces
1½ pounds boneless pork loin, cut into 2-inch chunks
2 sweet Italian sausages, sliced
½ teaspoon salt and pepper or to taste
1 bay leaf
2 tablespoons flour
1 cup dry white wine
1 cup water

In a Dutch oven, heat butter and oil and sauté onion, carrots, and
celery about 5 minutes. Remove with slotted spoon and set aside.
Add pork and sausage and sauté about 25 minutes or until brown.
Add salt, pepper, bay leaf, and flour, mixing well. Add wine and
water and bring to a boil, stirring. Cover and simmer for 1½ hours
or until pork is tender. Add reserved vegetables during last 30 minutes of cooking, stirring well. Serve with herb biscuits and cabbage.

Peggy Dunn
Fort Worth

W**e have so much warm weather in Texas that I rarely cook stew. However, when a Texas "Blue Norther" blows in, I have an excuse to cook something hot and heavy! This is one of my favorite cold-weather recipes.**

Anne's Blue Norther Meatball Stew

MEATBALLS
1 pound bulk pork sausage (hot)
1 pound ground chuck
½ cup bread crumbs
¼ cup chopped fresh parsley
½ cup minced onion
1 tablespoon catsup
flour
¼ cup oil
8 small, unpeeled new potatoes
4 carrots, halved

GRAVY
1 tablespoon flour
¼ teaspoon garlic powder
¼ teaspoon oregano
⅛ teaspoon salt
⅛ teaspoon black pepper
1 small can tomato sauce
1¼ cups water

Mix sausage, ground chuck, bread crumbs, parsley, onion, and catsup and mix well. Form into meatballs and roll in flour. Heat oil in a heavy skillet and brown meatballs. Transfer to a heavy Dutch oven. To make gravy, reheat oil in skillet and stir in flour. Add remaining ingredients. Stir until well mixed and pour over meatballs. Add potatoes and carrots, cover, and bake for 1 hour at 350 degrees. Serves 4.

Anne Teague
Mesquite

Pork Tenderloin

1 whole pork tenderloin
salt and pepper to taste
mustard
4 or more slices of bacon
pastry for one pie crust
1 egg yolk, diluted with water

Sprinkle tenderloin with salt and pepper. Smear with mustard and marinate 1 hour. Wrap bacon around tenderloin, overlapping edges. Roll out pastry and brush with egg yolk. Place tenderloin on top of pastry and roll up. Seal by brushing with egg yolk. Bake at 350 degrees until browned. Slice before serving.

Maurine S. Brief
Boerne

New Mexico Posole

1 large pork roast
1 32-ounce package frozen posole (uncooked hominy)
6 cans tomato sauce
3 teaspoons oregano
2 tablespoons garlic salt
1 ounce chili powder or to taste
water

Cook pork roast until well done, reserving broth. Cover frozen posole with water and boil over medium heat about 2 hours or until corn skin pops open. Rinse. Dice meat and combine with posole in large Dutch oven. Add reserved broth, tomato sauce, oregano, garlic salt, and chili powder. Add water to cover and simmer 20 minutes.

Carol Wallace
Amarillo

Carne de Puerco con Calabaza (Pork Steak with Squash)

½ to 2 pounds pork steak, trimmed and cubed
2 tablespoons cooking oil or shortening
1 small onion, diced
1 yellow squash, sliced
1 8-ounce can tomato sauce plus 1 can water
dash of garlic salt or garlic powder
salt and pepper to taste
1 16-ounce can whole-kernel corn, partially drained

Heat oil in a skillet, add meat, and cook until brown. Add onion and squash and sauté until tender, stirring constantly. Drain off excess oil and add tomato sauce plus water; mix well. Add seasonings, stir well, lower heat, and simmer for 3 minutes. Stir in corn and simmer 10 minutes more.

Mrs. Lupe S. Mercado
Fort Worth

When we asked our three-year-old son (who loves to eat) what he'd like for a birthday present, he said, "Posole!"

Catorce is what my Mexican baby-sitter called this dish. That was over fifty years ago, when I was a child, so I have never been able to find out how she came to call it by this name—which is the Spanish word for fourteen. For convenience my mother changed some of the ingredients over the years, more or less just throwing in whatever she had on hand. This is how we make Catorce now.

Catorce

½ pound bacon
1 pound smoked sausage, sliced thin
1 onion, peeled and chopped
2 cloves garlic, minced
2 bell peppers, chopped
2 stalks of celery, chopped
12 to 15 fresh mushrooms, washed and sliced
2 tablespoons butter or margarine
1½ cups lean diced ham
½ teaspoon salt
¾ teaspoon chili powder
¼ teaspoon cayenne pepper
⅓ teaspoon black pepper
1 tablespoon Tabasco sauce or more to taste
½ cup soy sauce
2 cups beef broth
1 cup water
1½ cups uncooked rice

Fry bacon in a large deep skillet until crisp. Remove, crumble, and set aside. In the same skillet brown sausage slices on both sides, remove, and set aside. In same skillet combine onion, garlic, bell peppers, celery, and mushrooms and cook until soft, stirring occasionally and adding butter or margarine if needed. Add ham and reserved bacon and sausage; cover and cook over low heat for 10 minutes. Mix remaining ingredients except rice and add to meat mixture. Stir well and bring to a boil. Add rice, lower heat, and simmer for 20 to 30 minutes.

Gene Stafford
Lamesa

Lemon-Baked Pork Chops

6 or 8 center-cut pork chops
1 cup flour
salt and pepper to taste
garlic powder
juice of 1 large lemon

Dredge pork chops in flour and place in baking dish. Sprinkle with salt, pepper, garlic powder, and lemon juice. Bake at 350 degrees for 1 hour or until done.

Mary Ann Currie
Franklin

Pork Chop Casserole

4 lean pork chops
oil
4 slices of onion
4 to 8 slices of cheddar cheese
½ cup canned or fresh mushrooms (optional)
1 can cream of mushroom soup
cooked rice

Trim all excess fat from pork chops and brown in oil. Place half the chops in a lightly oiled casserole dish, and top each chop with onion slice, cheese, mushrooms, and soup. Cover with layer of remaining chops and top with remaining onion, cheese, mushrooms, and soup. Pour any remaining soup over chops and bake uncovered at 350 degrees for 1 hour. Serve over rice. Serves 2.

Mrs. Frank Cole
Dallas

Wild Chinese Rice and Chops

1 6- or 8-ounce package long-grain and wild rice
1 can mushroom soup mixed with 1½ cups water
1 16-ounce can Chinese vegetables, drained
black pepper to taste
1 small can button mushrooms
1 can water chestnuts
6 lean pork chops

Combine rice, soup, and water in a 2-quart casserole dish. Add remaining ingredients and arrange pork chops on top. Bake at 350 degrees for 1 hour and 20 minutes. Serve with Chinese noodles and soy sauce.

E. A. "Mac" McBride
Brownwood

E. A. "Mac" McBride is a member of the Hadacol Angels, a motorcycle club for senior citizens.

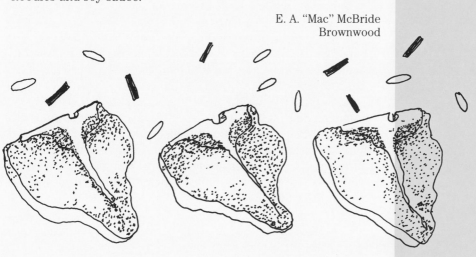

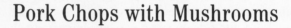

Pork Chops with Mushrooms

1 pound fresh mushrooms
6 tablespoons butter or margarine, divided
¾ cup chopped onion
1 cup bread crumbs
2 tablespoons chopped parsley
½ teaspoon salt
⅛ teaspoon black pepper
6 center-cut pork chops (1 inch thick)
2 tablespoons oil
1 beef bouillon cube
½ cup boiling water
½ teaspoon rosemary
1 tablespoon flour
1 cup sour cream
2 10-ounce packages frozen leaf spinach, cooked and drained

Remove mushroom caps from stems. Slice caps and set aside.
Chop stems and set aside. In a medium skillet, melt 3 tablespoons
butter. Add onions and sauté 2 minutes. Stir in reserved mushroom stems and sauté 2 minutes longer. Add bread crumbs, parsley, salt, and pepper. With a sharp knife cut a pocket in each
chop. Divide mushroom mixture equally and stuff into each pork
chop, securing with toothpicks. In a large skillet heat oil. Add
chops and sauté 5 minutes on each side or until brown. Dissolve
bouillon cube in boiling water and add to skillet. Sprinkle chops
with rosemary. Bring to a boil, reduce heat, cover, and simmer
about 45 minutes or until chops are tender. Melt remaining butter in a medium skillet. Add reserved mushroom caps and sauté
2 minutes. Remove chops and transfer mushroom caps to pork
chop liquid, cooking and stirring until thickened. Mix flour with
sour cream. Stir into mushroom mixture. Return chops to skillet,
cover, and simmer for 5 minutes. Serve over cooked spinach,
topped with sauce. Serves 6.

Sharon Privett
Bryan

Rice and Pork Chops

4 pork chops
salt and pepper
¼ cup chopped onions
¼ cup sliced celery
2 tablespoons vegetable oil
1½ cups water
2 tablespoons brown sugar
2 8-ounce can tomato sauce
1 cup rice

Sprinkle chops with salt and pepper. In a skillet lightly brown chops in oil; remove and set aside. Sauté onions and celery until soft. Add water, brown sugar, and tomato sauce and stir. Reduce heat, return chops to skillet, cover, and simmer 45 minutes. Serves 4.

Alta L. Westerfeld
Houston

Corn and Sausage Skillet Bake

1 pound sausage
1 17-ounce can cream-style corn
1 tablespoon diced onion
1 tablespoon margarine
½ teaspoon salt
½ teaspoon pepper
1 small jar chopped pimientos
1 7½-ounce package yellow cornbread mix

Cook sausage in a 10-inch cast iron skillet until crumbly and well done. Add remaining ingredients except cornbread mix. Simmer 10 minutes. Prepare cornbread mix as directed on package. Spread evenly on top of corn mixture. Bake at 400 degrees for 20 to 25 minutes or until golden brown. Serves 4 to 6.

Sue Richie McSpadden
Frankston

My recipe was the first-prize winner in a contest sponsored by Pride of Illinois Golden Sweet Cream-Style Corn and was featured in the November 1984 issue of *Southern Living* magazine.

Potato-Sausage Casserole

1 pound pork sausage
1 can mushroom soup
¾ cup milk
½ cup chopped onion
½ teaspoon salt
¼ teaspoon pepper
3 cups sliced potatoes
butter
½ pound grated cheese

Brown and drain sausage. Mix soup, milk, onion, salt, and pepper. In a large casserole dish, layer potatoes, soup mixture, and sausage. Repeat, ending with sausage layer. Dot with butter. Bake covered at 350 degrees for 1¼ to 1½ hours. Sprinkle with grated cheese and return to oven; heat until cheese is melted.

Hortense Phillips
Lockney

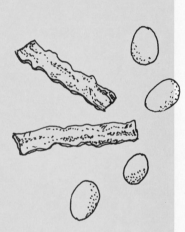

Milton Watts runs a fishing camp on Lake O' The Pines in the piney woods of East Texas.

Island View Landing Breakfast

During the last thirty years at Island View Landing on Lake O' The Pines, breakfast for dock hands and fishermen has become almost automatic. It's merely a matter of getting at it by about four o'clock in the morning.

Start by baking a big batch of biscuits, then slicing huge platters of ham and bacon, which is fried in a big cast iron skillet on a hot stove. When the meat is done, save the drippings and dump in bowls of scrambled eggs and add some milk and warm water, then stir like hell. The eggs will hit the plates fluffy and tasty. Prepare a side order of gravy from the ham and bacon drippings; just add flour, milk, salt, and black pepper. You'll arrive at the right consistency and taste as you add and stir. Don't forget to fry some potatoes to pour the gravy over and complement the eggs. Saucers of sliced tomatoes, onions, and pickled jalapeño peppers will add even more excitement to the breakfast.

Don't worry about cholesterol! Just look forward to the hard work and good fishing you'll be doing after breakfast.

Good health through good eating and energetic endeavor from Island View Landing, Lake O' The Pines.

Geraldine Allen
Marilyn, Nettie, and Milton Watts
Jefferson

Ham Tetrazzini

1 8-ounce package thin spaghetti
1 6-ounce jar sliced mushrooms
1 small onion, chopped
¼ cup margarine
¼ cup flour
½ teaspoon dry mustard
1½ cups milk
1 teaspoon chicken bouillon granules
1 teaspoon Worcestershire sauce
2 cups diced cooked ham
salt and pepper to taste
½ cup grated Parmesan cheese

Cook spaghetti. Drain and set aside. Drain mushrooms and save the liquid. Add water to mushroom liquid to equal 1 cup. Set aside. In medium saucepan sauté onion in margarine until onion is clear. Add flour and dry mustard, stirring until smooth. Cook 1 minute, stirring constantly. Gradually add mushroom liquid, milk, bouillon granules, and Worcestershire sauce. Cook, stirring constantly, until thick and bubbly. Combine cooked spaghetti, reserved mushrooms, ham, and salt and pepper. Spoon mixture into a buttered 2-quart shallow baking dish. Cover and refrigerate several hours or overnight. Remove from refrigerator and let stand 30 minutes. Bake covered at 350 degrees for 30 minutes. Uncover and bake 5 minutes more. Sprinkle with Parmesan cheese and bake 10 minutes uncovered.

Louise Clark
El Campo

Sausage

12 pounds ground pork
3 tablespoons salt
2 tablespoons black pepper
½ tablespoon cayenne pepper
3 tablespoons sage

Mix thoroughly and put in sacks made from muslin.

Laura Lee Adams
Claude

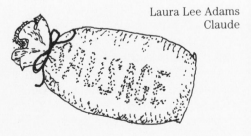

When I was a little girl, we usually butchered hogs the day after Christmas—when the weather was usually cold enough to keep the meat from spoiling. The sausage was my favorite part, and I still use this recipe to make sausage, even though we have the butchering done.

Laura Lee Adams has spent her entire life in the vicinity of Palo Duro Canyon. She runs the farm bureau in Claude and in her spare time creates sculpture from horseshoe nails.

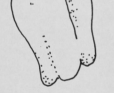

This recipe is straight
from the old oil patch.

Midnight Tour Lunch

1 long link sausage
1 Irish potato or sweet potato
1 onion

Wrap ingredients in paper sack or butcher paper, then wrap in newspaper. Place on top of boiler (100 pounds of steam = 350 degree oven). When bit is turning to the right, remove and unwrap and—lunch!

Grover Q. Poole
Dallas

GAME

Dove Dinner

16 to 24 dove breasts, boned or unboned
¼ pound butter
½ cup oil
1 medium white or yellow onion, diced
2 cloves garlic, crushed
1 can beef broth
1 can Campbell's French Onion soup
1 cup sliced green onions, with tops
2 bell peppers, cut into strips
1 4-ounce can mushrooms
2 tablespoons cornstarch
⅓ cup soy sauce mixed with ⅓ cup water
1 can peeled tomatoes, drained and quartered

Soak doves in vinegar and water overnight or use fresh. In a very large skillet, brown doves and white or yellow onion in butter and oil. Add garlic, broth, and soup; cover and let simmer for 30 minutes. Stir in green onions, bell peppers, and mushrooms; cover and cook 5 minutes more. Blend cornstarch, soy sauce, and water, then stir into skillet mixture. Cook, stirring, about 2 minutes or until clear and thickened. Add tomatoes, stirring gently until tomatoes are coated with sauce. Serves 6 to 8.

VARIATIONS

Venison or round steak: Pound meat ¼ inch thick and cut into ½-inch-wide strips. Sprinkle with paprika, and allow to stand. Omit onion soup, but add 1 additional can of beef broth. Serve over fluffy rice.

Spareribs: Prepare as in dove recipe, but salt and pepper ribs before starting to cook. Add ⅔ cup brown sugar along with green onions and bell peppers.

Gene Stafford
Lamesa

Ostrich Stroganoff

flour seasoned with ½ teaspoon salt
1 pound ostrich or sirloin, cut into strips
2 teaspoons butter
1 cup mushrooms
1½ cups onion
1 clove garlic, minced
2 tablespoons butter
3 tablespoons flour
1½ cups beef stock or 1 can condensed beef broth
1 cup sour cream

Dredge meat in seasoned flour. Heat 2 teaspoons butter in skillet and brown ostrich quickly on all sides. Add mushrooms, onion, and garlic. Cook 3 or 4 minutes or until onion is barely tender. Remove meat and mushrooms and set aside. Add 2 tablespoons butter to pan drippings and blend in 3 tablespoons flour. Slowly pour in cold meat stock. Cook and stir until thickened. Return meat and mushrooms to skillet. Stir in sour cream. Serve over parsley rice or hot buttered noodles. Serves 6.

Don and Bonnie Hall
Quail

Don and Bonnie Hall operate the Quail Ostrich Farm, one of the first such farms established in the state.

Chicken-Fried Venison Steak

venison backstrap, cut into 1-inch steaks
2 eggs, lightly beaten
½ cup milk
flour
oil

Mix together eggs and milk. Dip steaks into egg and milk mixture and dredge in flour. Heat oil and fry steaks over medium heat for 10 to 12 minutes.

Jayne Smith
McKinney

Ledesma's Deer Jerky

1 cup coffee
1 cup teriyaki sauce
½ cup soy sauce
1 tablespoon monosodium glutamate
½ cup Worcestershire sauce
¼ cup Liquid Smoke
1 tablespoon black pepper
3 tablespoons cayenne pepper
2 tablespoons garlic powder
1 tablespoon seasoned salt
3 pounds deer meat, cut into strips or chunks
coarse-ground black pepper

Mix first ten ingredients to make a marinade. Soak meat, refrigerated, in the marinade overnight or up to 24 hours. Drain well. Coat with coarse-ground black pepper. Line the bottom of the oven with foil. Spear meat with toothpicks and hang from the oven rack. Set oven at 150 degrees. Keep oven door ajar to help the meat dry. (This can also be done in a dehydrator.)

Mary Ellen Ledesma
Bertram

German Steaks

1½ pounds venison steaks or round steak
bacon strips
dill pickles, sliced thick lengthwise
1 teaspoon salt
pepper to taste
flour
vegetable oil
1½ cups water
½ cup catsup
2 tablespoons Worcestershire sauce

Cut steak into serving-size pieces; lay strip of bacon on each piece and a slice of pickle on top of bacon. Roll up and secure with toothpicks. Sprinkle with salt and pepper and cover with flour, then brown in oil. Place in a casserole dish. Mix together water, catsup, and Worcestershire sauce and pour over rolls. Cover and bake at 350 degrees for 1½ hours.

Virginia Hatcher Huth
Ponca City

Mexican Cornbread with Hot Sauce

1 pound ground venison
1 large onion, chopped
1½ tablespoons chili powder
1 teaspoon salt
½ teaspoon garlic salt
1 cup flour
1 cup yellow cornmeal
3 teaspoons baking powder
¾ teaspoon salt
1 egg
1 cup milk
¼ cup soft margarine
2 to 3 jalapeño peppers, diced and seeded
1 cup sharp cheddar cheese, grated
1 No. 303 can cream-style corn

HOT SAUCE
5 to 6 slices bacon
½ large onion, chopped
2 cans Ro-tel tomatoes, diced

Brown ground meat and onion, then drain. Add chili powder, salt, and garlic salt. Set aside. Mix remaining ingredients. Heat and grease a 10-inch cast iron skillet. Pour half of cornbread batter into skillet. Cover with meat mixture and then remaining cornbread batter. Bake at 400 degrees for about 30 minutes.

To make hot sauce, fry bacon until crisp; drain and crumble. In small amount of bacon grease, cook onion until transparent. Add bacon and tomatoes. Simmer until flavors are blended. Serve hot over wedges of cornbread.

Levonne Overstreet
Weatherford

Venison Casserole

1 pound ground venison or ground beef
butter
1 medium onion, chopped
1¼ cups chopped celery
1½ cups cooked Uncle Ben's wild rice
1 can cream of mushroom soup
1 can cream of chicken soup
1 cup sliced mushrooms
1 cup water
4 tablespoons soy sauce

Brown venison, then sauté onion and celery in butter until tender. Mix all ingredients together and bake, covered, at 350 degrees for 30 minutes; remove cover and bake an additional 30 minutes. Serve with a side dish of broccoli.

Debbie Bender
Brenham

This recipe is as easily prepared in the deer camp as in your own kitchen. Venison is low in cholesterol and fats but high in protein.

Sulphur River Squirrel Stew

3 large full-grown squirrels or 3 pounds beef
6 medium potatoes
2 medium onions
2 small cans Ro-tel tomatoes and green chilies
2 No. 202 cans Veg-All
2 No. 202 cans tomato juice
½ cup elbow macaroni
1 16-ounce jar picante sauce
4 tablespoons paprika
4 tablespoons chili powder
salt and pepper to taste

Cover meat with water and cook until tender. Add potatoes and onions and cook approximately 30 minutes. Add remaining ingredients and cook until macaroni is done. Serves 6 to 12.

W. D. Holt
Sugarhill

This stew is best when cooked over a campfire and served to hungry hunters or fishermen.

W. D. Holt, nicknamed "Chainsaw Willie," uses a chainsaw to create art from Northeast Texas pine trees.

Texas Rattlesnake Chili

2 tablespoons oil
½ cup chopped onion
½ cup chopped bell pepper
1 clove garlic, minced
1 pound lean ground beef
1 cup cubed rattlesnake meat or chicken
2 teaspoons salt
1 teaspoon cayenne pepper
2 16-ounce cans tomatoes, undrained
1 6-ounce can tomato paste
2 cups water
2 cups Skinner Lone Star Pasta, uncooked

In 5-quart saucepan or Dutch oven, heat oil and sauté onion, bell pepper, and garlic until tender but not brown. Add ground beef and rattlesnake meat; brown and cook 5 minutes or until done. Stir in salt, cayenne pepper, tomatoes, and tomato paste. Bring to a boil, then reduce heat and simmer about 2 hours. Add water and return to a boil. Stir in uncooked pasta; continue boiling, stirring frequently, 10 to 15 minutes or until pasta is tender. Serves 6.

DRESSING RATTLESNAKES
1. Place dead rattlesnake on a cutting board and hold firmly behind the head.
2. Cut off head and rattles and discard.
3. Strip off skin and discard or save (for a hat band, for example).
4. Make a long slice along the underside and remove all internal organs.
5. Cut into chunks and refrigerate or freeze until ready to use.

Kenneth Carr
Amarillo

124

Waterfowl and Dressing

1 wild goose or 2 wild ducks
1 large apple, sliced
4 ribs celery, sliced
1 small onion, chopped
4 slices of bacon

DRESSING
1 8-ounce package fresh mushrooms, sliced
¼ cup margarine
½ cup water
1 tablespoon Worcestershire sauce
1 cup consommé
1 cup Bing cherries
1 tablespoon lemon juice
1 tablespoon lemon peel, grated
½ cup currant jelly or tart cherry jelly
6 to 8 ounces almond slivers
1 tablespoon parsley
3 cups cooked white rice
3 cups cooked brown wild rice

Thoroughly clean fowl and stuff with apple, celery, and onion. Place in a roaster and lay bacon over fowl. Cook at 350 degrees for 1 hour. Remove from oven and drain off excess liquid, then remove apple mixture. To make dressing, sauté mushrooms in margarine, water, and Worcestershire sauce until tender. Add consommé, cherries and their juice, lemon juice, lemon peel, jelly, and parsley. Simmer for 30 minutes, stirring occasionally. Add almonds and simmer 10 minutes more. Transfer to a large bowl and mix in rices. Stuff bird cavity with dressing, using excess dressing as a bed for the bird. Return to oven and cook for 30 minutes or until breast is tender.

Jim Kepley
Amarillo

SAUCES

Mother Zedler's Barbecue Sauce

¾ cup vinegar
½ cup water
⅓ cup sugar
3 tablespoons prepared mustard
½ teaspoon black pepper
1½ teaspoons salt
½ teaspoon cayenne pepper
1 large lemon, sliced, or 2 tablespoons lemon juice concentrate
1 medium onion, sliced, or 2 tablespoons onion powder
½ cup butter or margarine (plus ¼ cup for fowl; plus ½ cup for fish)
¼ tablespoon Worcestershire sauce

Combine first nine ingredients in a 2-quart saucepan. Simmer over low heat for 20 minutes. Then add remaining ingredients and simmer another 20 minutes. Makes about 2½ cups. Good with all meats, game, fowl, and fish.

Mrs. A. L. Zedler
Liberty Hill

Harold's and K. D.'s Barbecue Sauce

1¼ cups tomato juice
1 cup catsup
¼ cup Worcestershire sauce
juice of 1 lemon
1½ sticks margarine
1 clove garlic, crushed
¾ teaspoon Tabasco sauce
1½ teaspoons chili powder
⅛ teaspoon paprika
¼ teaspoon salt
¼ teaspoon pepper
1½ teaspoons brown sugar

Combine all ingredients. Simmer 20 minutes and serve while warm.

Joe Michael Feist
Lancaster

Harold Franke, a barbecue aficionado in Rowena, came up with the basis for this sauce in the 1930s and 1940s. It was further refined over the years by my father, K. D. Feist, of Rowena. This is a good recipe to play with— try more or less lemon juice, Tabasco sauce, and seasonings. You can't go wrong.

This is the recipe for the barbecue sauce used at the St. Anne's Catholic Church picnics at Rosebud in the early 1960s. My mother used to make the sauce in a large black pot over an open fire in the backyard. The recipe was increased ten times.

Barbecue Sauce

1 stick butter
2 large onions, chopped
1 clove garlic, minced, or garlic powder
2 8-ounce cans tomato sauce
4 cups water
2 small (approximately 12-ounce) bottles of catsup
3 teaspoons salt
2 teaspoons black pepper
3 tablespoons sugar
5 tablespoons Worcestershire sauce
4 tablespoons vinegar
few drops of Tabasco sauce
1 tablespoon chili powder

Cook butter, onions, and garlic in a large skillet until soft. Add remaining ingredients. Taste to correct seasonings and simmer uncovered for 30 minutes to 1 hour. Makes 1 gallon.

Marla Wallace
Rosebud

Beef or Venison Marinade

½ cup soy sauce or Worcestershire sauce
¼ cup sugar
¼ cup vinegar
½ teaspoon black pepper
½ teaspoon garlic powder
¼ teaspoon ginger

Mix all ingredients. Pour over meat and soak at least 15 minutes per side (but the longer, the better).

Deidra Meiron
Stephenville

FISH & SEAFOOD

Blackened Fish Fillets

1 tablespoon paprika
1 teaspoon salt
1 teaspoon onion powder
1 teaspoon garlic powder
¾ teaspoon black pepper
¾ teaspoon white pepper
½ teaspoon cayenne pepper
½ teaspoon dried thyme
½ teaspoon oregano
2 pounds fish fillets
1 cup margarine or butter

Mix all dry ingredients in a shallow pan and set aside. Heat a large cast iron skillet over high heat (do not use a lightweight or nonstick skillet). Turn on hood vent. Melt margarine in skillet and transfer all but about 3 tablespoons to a shallow dish. Dip fish in reserved melted margarine, then coat with reserved dry ingredients, patting them into fish by hand. Cook fish on each side for 2 or 3 minutes, turning carefully. The fish will look charred, and there will be some smoke. The fish can be cooked outdoors if preferred. Serves 5 to 6.

Ima Ray Watson
Leona

Baked Catfish

For this dish, I use any fish my husband catches.

2 pounds catfish, boned and cut into bite-size pieces
salt and pepper to taste
2 cups cooked rice
2 tablespoons grated onion
½ teaspoon curry powder
6 thin lemon slices
¼ cup butter or margarine
chopped parsley

Place fish in a well-greased 13″ × 9″ × 2″ baking dish. Sprinkle with salt and pepper. Combine rice, onion, and curry powder and spread over fish. Top with lemon and dot with butter. Bake covered at 350 degrees for 25 to 30 minutes. Uncover and let fish brown for a few minutes. Sprinkle with parsley. Serves 6.

Lorraine Killian
Denton

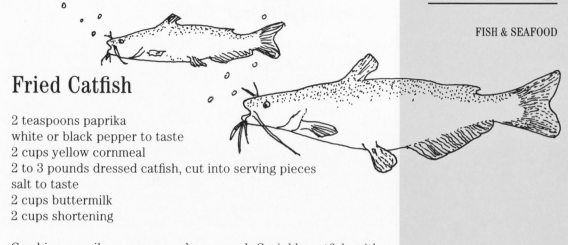

Fried Catfish

2 teaspoons paprika
white or black pepper to taste
2 cups yellow cornmeal
2 to 3 pounds dressed catfish, cut into serving pieces
salt to taste
2 cups buttermilk
2 cups shortening

Combine paprika, pepper, and cornmeal. Sprinkle catfish with salt. Dip catfish in buttermilk, then roll in seasoned cornmeal. Heat shortening in heavy skillet and fry catfish until golden brown. Drain on paper towels. Serves 4.

Sam Morris
Fort Worth

Cheesy Flounder Fillets

⅓ cup yogurt cheese
1½ pounds flounder fillets
vegetable oil spray
2 teaspoons cornstarch
2 tablespoons grated Parmesan cheese
2 tablespoons fresh parsley
¼ cup minced onion
1 tablespoon lemon juice
1 tablespoon fresh dill or 1 teaspoon dried dill (or tarragon or marjoram)
cayenne pepper to taste (optional)

To make yogurt cheese, fit the mouth of a funnel with fine-weave cheesecloth (or use a yogurt cheese funnel). Pour yogurt which contains no stabilizer or gelatin base into funnel and rest funnel over a glass or cup to catch the whey. Refrigerate and let drain 8 to 10 hours. Arrange fillets in a 9″ × 13″ baking pan sprayed with vegetable oil. Combine remaining ingredients and spread mixture evenly over fillets. Sprinkle with cayenne pepper. Bake at 350 degrees for 15 minutes or until fish flakes easily. If desired, place under broiler for 1 to 2 minutes or until cheese mixture begins to brown.

Carol Barclay
Portland

Greek-Style Crappie

2 tablespoons olive oil
1 clove garlic, minced
1 tablespoon basil
1 cup fresh tomatoes, diced
½ cup ripe olives, cut in half
2 tablespoons lemon juice
¼ teaspoon pepper
¼ cup dry white wine
1 pound crappie fillets, cut into 1-inch pieces
¼ pound feta cheese, crumbled
¼ cup fresh chives, chopped

Combine oil, garlic, basil, tomatoes, olives, lemon juice, and pepper and heat in a skillet over medium-high heat for about 5 minutes. Add wine and fish pieces and cook for about 5 more minutes or until fish turns opaque. Remove from heat and stir in cheese and chives. Makes 4 servings.

Fred L. Jisha
Yantis

Fred's Fried Fish

½ cup honey
2 tablespoons cayenne pepper
1½ tablespoons salt
½ tablespoon celery salt
1 6-ounce bottle Evangeline Louisiana Red Hot Sauce
1 quart buttermilk
juice of 2 lemons
2 pounds fish fillets
vegetable oil

Combine honey, cayenne pepper, salt, and celery salt in bowl and microwave until honey is thin. While still warm, add hot sauce, buttermilk, and lemon juice, mixing well. Add fish fillets and marinate for 2 hours in refrigerator. Drain fillets and coat with seasoned cornmeal. Heat oil in a Dutch oven to a depth of 4 inches and fry fish over high heat until fish floats. Drain on newspaper. Salt to taste. Serve hot.

Fred Harrington
Duncanville

Puffed Salmon Croquettes

½ cup milk
2 eggs
½ cup buttermilk
salt to taste
1 teaspoon baking soda
2 tablespoons baking powder
½ cup flour
1 large can salmon

Mix all ingredients together in order listed. Form balls using a teaspoon and drop balls into hot grease. Flatten slightly and fry until golden. Drain and serve hot.

Samantha Lush
Cleburne

Salmon Soufflé

3 tablespoons vegetable oil
5 or 6 slices white bread, made into crumbs
1 15½-ounce can salmon, drained and flaked with skin and
    bones removed
½ cup milk
3 eggs, separated
3 tablespoons lemon juice
¼ cup fine-grated onion
¼ teaspoon salt
pepper to taste
paprika

In a bowl combine all ingredients except egg whites and paprika. Beat egg whites until stiff. Fold into salmon mixture. Pour into a lightly oiled loaf pan and sprinkle with paprika. Bake uncovered at 300 degrees for about 1 hour, or until puffed and lightly browned. Serves 4 to 6.

Melba Anderson
Granbury

Willard's Tuna Stuff

4 cans tuna, drained
1 medium onion, chopped fine
¼ cup jalapeños, chopped
⅛ cup Longhorn cheese, grated

Mix tuna, onion, and jalapeños to form layer about 1 inch thick in a baking dish. Top with cheese. Bake at 375 degrees about 20 minutes or until cheese is melted and slightly brown. Serves 4 to 6.

Willard Deason
Valley Mills

Tuna-Macaroni Casserole

2 cups large elbow macaroni, uncooked
1 10½-ounce can mushroom soup
1 cup milk
1 tablespoon chopped onion
1 tablespoon chopped pimiento
2 tablespoons chopped bell pepper
¼ teaspoon black pepper
¼ pound processed sharp cheddar cheese, grated or cubed
1 6½-ounce can tuna, drained

Cook macaroni according to directions on package. Drain and set aside. Combine all remaining ingredients except cheese and mix. Heat over low heat, add grated cheese, and stir occasionally until cheese is melted. Mix in macaroni and transfer to a 1½-quart casserole dish. Bake at 325 degrees for about 20 minutes.

Lola Miller
Lubbock

White Clam Sauce

1 tablespoon butter
½ pint cream
2 tablespoons flour
2 tablespoons cornstarch
1 tablespoon butter
½ cup white wine
¾ cup chicken broth
2 cloves garlic, minced
½ cup fine-chopped onion
2 tablespoons sweet basil
1 tablespoon parsley flakes
pepper to taste
1 10-ounce can clams
½ teaspoon lemon juice

Combine butter, cream, and flour in a saucepan and cook until thick. Set aside. In a separate saucepan, combine all remaining ingredients except clams and lemon juice. Cook until thick. Add clams, lemon juice, and reserved cream sauce. Add milk if necessary for desired consistency. Serve over pasta.

Sarah L. Helford
Dallas

Smoked Sausage and Oysters

2 pounds country-smoked sausage, cut into 1-inch pieces
1 or 2 cloves garlic
1 quart medium oysters
2 cups sauterne wine
1 teaspoon Tabasco sauce
½ teaspoon salt
juice from ½ lemon

In a large cast iron skillet, lightly brown sausage. Add garlic and cook until sausage is brown and well done. Add remaining ingredients and bring to a boil. Lower heat and simmer until most of the liquid is evaporated. Serve remaining liquid as gravy if desired. Serves 6 to 8.

Judy Kilpatrick
Kerrville

As a young girl growing up in Corpus Christi, my mother frequently fixed this smoked sausage and oyster dish when my aunts, uncles, and cousins from around Texas gathered at our house for family get-togethers. I didn't realize it then, but the origin of the recipe must be Cajun because as a young wife living in Louisiana, I discovered a similar dish. I most often use it as an appetizer. It's especially good when served with crusty French bread to sop up all of the tasty sauce!

Here's a recipe my father created. His favorite pastime was fishing or bringing home oysters while living in Galveston.

Oyster Loaf

1 large loaf French bread
2 to 3 dozen oysters, rinsed, drained, and dredged in cornmeal
salt and pepper to taste
1 stick butter
1 stalk celery, diced
1 large onion, diced
1 tablespoon parsley flakes
juice of 1 lemon
catsup
dill pickle relish (optional)

Slice bread in half lengthwise. Scoop out most of the bread and set halves aside. Fry oysters until crisp and sprinkle with salt and pepper. Set aside. Melt butter and sauté celery and onion until soft. Add parsley flakes. Fill bottom half of French bread with oysters, followed by a layer of the onion and celery mixture. Sprinkle with lemon juice and spread catsup evenly over the top. Cover with top half of French bread and wrap loaf in foil. Heat at 300 degrees until warm. Slice in large pieces with a bread knife. Serve warm with dill pickle relish.

Marjorie Finney
Texas City

Shrimp Stingo

1 12-ounce package frozen raw shrimp, peeled and deveined
1 small onion, chopped
2 cloves garlic, minced
1 teaspoon salt
1 teaspoon black pepper
½ teaspoon cayenne pepper
½ teaspoon seasoned pepper
½ teaspoon thyme
¼ cup chopped fresh parsley (or 1 tablespoon dried parsley)
1 tablespoon olive oil
1 tablespoon Worcestershire sauce

Combine all ingredients except butter and mix well. Cover and refrigerate at least 2 hours, stirring occasionally. When ready to serve, remove shrimp from marinade. Melt butter in a skillet and sauté shrimp over medium-high heat until done. Serve over cooked rice seasoned with butter, salt, and pepper. Serves 3.

Ellen A. Lloyd
Aransas Pass

Crab Muffins

1 6-ounce package chicken-flavored stuffing mix
2 cups water
1½ cups fine-chopped celery
1½ cups fine-chopped onion
1 cup chopped bell pepper
1 can cream of mushroom soup, undiluted
2 eggs, beaten
1 cup crabmeat, packed

Boil water and seasoning for stuffing mix for 2 minutes. Add stuffing, mix lightly, and set aside. Sauté celery, onion, and bell pepper until soft and set aside. Combine undiluted soup, eggs, and crabmeat. Add reserved stuffing mixture and sautéed vegetables and mix well. Spoon into greased muffin tins and bake at 375 degrees for 20 minutes. Makes 18 muffins.

Ellen John
San Leon

Stewed Shrimp

2 tablespoons butter
1 tablespoon flour
2 onions, minced
1¼ cups tomatoes, chopped
1 cup water
1 bell pepper, chopped
½ teaspoon thyme
1 tablespoon parsley
1 bay leaf, broken into pieces
½ teaspoon garlic salt
salt and pepper to taste
red pepper sauce to taste
2 pounds raw shrimp, shelled and deveined
cooked white rice

In a large frying pan melt butter. Add flour and cook over medium heat until light brown, stirring constantly. Add all remaining ingredients except shrimp and rice and cook over medium heat, stirring often, for 10 minutes. Add shrimp and cook, stirring, for about 5 minutes, or until shrimp loses its transparency. Remove from heat and adjust seasonings. Serve immediately over rice.

Betty Outlaw
Sweeny

W hat makes these muffins so great is the time and love involved. I live in a small community almost surrounded by Galveston Bay. I sit on the pier, catch the crabs, clean the crabs, boil the crabs, pick the meat from the crabs, and the rest is easy. My family and friends just love the muffins. Of course, there's an easy way—buy the crabmeat at the market. I guess being retired, I have the time to start from scratch, and it also helps to have a bay full of crabs.

Seafood Gumbo for 25

1½ to 2 cups roux
2 gallons water or seafood stock
5 large onions, chopped
4 garlic pods, minced (or 1 tablespoon garlic powder)
6 large bell peppers, chopped
1 celery stalk, chopped
2 cups stewed okra and tomatoes (optional)
13 pounds shrimp, cleaned
1½ pounds crabmeat
salt to taste
black pepper to taste
cayenne pepper to taste
1 quart oysters (optional)
10 cups rice, cooked
chopped green onions
filé

ROUX
3 cups flour
1 cup oil

To make roux, combine flour and oil in an iron skillet and blend until smooth. Bake at 350 to 400 degrees until dark brown, stirring every 15 or 20 minutes and checking frequently to make sure roux does not burn. To make gumbo, transfer 1½ to 2 cups roux to a large gumbo pot and heat roux over medium heat. Add water, a small amount at a time, to dissolve roux. Cook 30 to 45 minutes, then add onions, garlic, bell pepper, and celery and cook until vegetables are done. Add cooked okra and tomatoes, shrimp, crabmeat, and seasonings and cook for about 20 minutes; then add oysters and cook for another 10 minutes. Adjust seasonings. Serve over rice and garnish with green onions and filé. Serves 25.

Marian Andrews
Beaumont

This is a recipe for gumbo that I've used for our family's Christmas dinner for several years. It has become a tradition for us. Since we live in Southeast Texas and have access to fresh seafood, we enjoy a break from the more traditional holiday fare.

Salmon Chowder

4 slices of bacon, diced
1 onion, diced
2 15-ounce cans pink salmon, undrained
1 14½-ounce can whole tomatoes, undrained
1 8-ounce can tomato sauce
3 medium potatoes, diced
2 ribs celery, diced
½ teaspoon oregano
2 bay leaves
2 teaspoons lemon juice
salt and pepper to taste

Fry bacon until crisp, drain, and set aside. Cook onion in bacon drippings until soft. Transfer to a 6-quart pot and add bacon and all remaining ingredients. Cover and cook over medium heat until potatoes are soft. Serve with French bread. Serves 8.

Marilyn Carter
Kerrville

Robert A. Kearley's Fishhead Chowder

head and backbone from snapper, flounder, or other fish
1 to 2 bay leaves
6 to 8 peppercorns
2 teaspoons salt, divided
3 cups water, divided
2 cups diced potatoes
¼ pound salt pork, diced
5 teaspoons flour
2 cups milk
salt
1 tomato, diced (optional)
minced parsley or paprika

This is a recipe I devised for using the parts of a fish that are usually discarded after filleting. It can be adapted for a small whole fish, fish fillets, or leftover fish.

Clean, scale, and rinse fish head. Rinse backbone. Simmer for about 30 minutes with bay leaves, peppercorns, and 1 teaspoon salt in 2 cups water or to cover. Remove fish, reserving liquid. Flake fish from bones, discarding bones. (There should be ½ cup fish.) Simmer potatoes with 1 teaspoon salt in 1 cup water or to barely cover and cook until done. In cast iron Dutch oven or other heavy pot render salt pork over medium-low heat until brown. Stir in enough flour to absorb rendered fat. Add milk, a little at a time, stirring to make a smooth sauce. Add potatoes and potato water, stirring. Add flaked fish, fish liquid, and tomato. Stir and heat until mixture reaches simmering stage and thickens. If needed, thicken with additional flour mixed with milk. Garnish with minced parsley or paprika. Serve with thin wheat crackers or saltines and Tabasco sauce if desired.

Robert A. Kearley
Corpus Christi

Spices for Blackened Fish or Chicken

2 teaspoons garlic salt
2 teaspoons paprika
1 teaspoon dried basil
1 teaspoon dry mustard
1 teaspoon dried thyme
1 teaspoon ground red pepper or to taste
2 teaspoons ground black pepper

Combine the spices in a bowl. Sprinkle over fish and press it into the flesh. Heat a heavy iron skillet very hot. Add the fish and cook approximately 10 minutes, turning once. Because no oil is used, this is very good for someone on a diet. (Note: Because of the smoke, I like to cook this outside using my camp stove.)

Ken Hillis
Rowlett

BREADS

The nice thing about these biscuits is that you can store the dough in the refrigerator and make it up as needed. Angel Biscuits are also ideal for camping trips.

Terrell's Ranch-Style Angel Biscuits

1 package dry yeast
¼ cup lukewarm water
2 cups flour
1 teaspoon baking powder
2 teaspoons sugar
½ teaspoon baking soda
1 teaspoon salt
3 tablespoons shortening
½ cup buttermilk

Soften yeast in lukewarm water and set aside. Sift dry ingredients together, then add milk and softened yeast, stirring until well blended. Store in refrigerator until 1 hour before baking. Roll out dough ½ inch thick and cut out using a 2-inch biscuit cutter. Bake at 450 degrees for 10 minutes or until light brown. Makes 24 biscuits.

For campfire baking, place biscuits in a well-greased cast iron Dutch oven. Cover and place a few white-hot coals on lid. Allow biscuits to rise 10 to 15 minutes. Replace coals on oven lid and let biscuits bake for about 20 minutes. Set Dutch oven on coals, spreading additional coals evenly around bottom of Dutch oven about 1 inch from sides. Replace coals as needed. Check every 5 minutes until biscuits are done.

Terrell Eastwood
Springtown

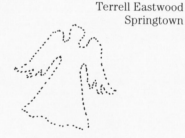

Milam Biscuits

1 quart milk
3 packages dry yeast
1 cup shortening, melted
½ cup sugar
9 to 11 cups flour
2 teaspoons salt
1 teaspoon baking soda
2 tablespoons baking powder

Scald milk, then set aside to cool until lukewarm. Sprinkle yeast over top. Let set 10 minutes. Transfer to a very large bowl; add shortening, sugar, and enough flour to make a thick batter (like cottage cheese). Cover with a damp cloth and let rise in a warm place until double in bulk. Stir in salt, soda, baking powder, and enough flour to handle easily (dough should be moist and somewhat sticky). Flour hands and knead 8 to 10 minutes or until dough pops and snaps. Return to bowl and let rise until double in bulk. (At this point dough can be stored in the refrigerator and used as needed over several days; or it can be rolled out and the biscuits cut out and frozen.) To bake, place biscuits on a greased cookie sheet and brush tops with melted butter. (If frozen, thaw and let rise slightly.) Bake at 450 degrees for 15 to 20 minutes or until lightly browned. Makes 60 to 85 biscuits.

Don Milam Brady
Lubbock

Onion Bread

1 cup milk, scalded
3 tablespoons sugar
½ teaspoon salt
1½ tablespoons butter
1 package dry yeast
¾ cup warm water
1 package onion soup mix
4 cups flour

In medium bowl mix milk, sugar, salt, and butter. Cool until lukewarm. Sprinkle yeast into water and stir until dissolved. Add yeast mixture to milk mixture, then add soup mix and flour. Stir and blend about 2 minutes. Cover and let rise in warm place about 45 minutes or until double. Stir down batter, beating ½ minute. Turn into a greased 1½-quart casserole dish. Bake uncovered at 375 degrees about 1 hour.

Evelyn Littleton
Euless

Skillet Bread

2 cups flour
4 teaspoons baking powder
2 teaspoons salt (optional)
1¼ cups milk
2 tablespoons butter or margarine

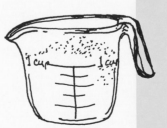

These biscuits won a blue ribbon at the West Texas Fair in Abilene. The recipe came from my mother, Mrs. Sim Murray of Big Lake, who got the recipe from her grandmother, Mrs. Thomas M. Milam, through her mother, Mrs. Tom McKenzie. Mrs. Thomas M. Milam was the daughter of W. W. (Fuzzy Buck) Arnett, an early Texas newspaper columnist. Her husband was the first judge of Uvalde.

Don Brady is the winemaker at Llano Estacado, where award-winning Texas wine is made from Texas-grown grapes.

Skillet bread has a place in history. Cooks who crossed the country in a Conestoga wagon knew how to prepare it whenever they could pull out their frying pans.

In a large bowl mix flour, baking powder, and salt. Add milk and stir with a wooden spoon until mixture is spongy. Heat butter in a 10-inch skillet over low heat; do not brown. Spread butter evenly over bottom of pan and add batter. Cook 15 minutes or until bottom is golden brown. Use a large spatula to lift and turn. Cook 15 minutes more. Turn out on a round platter and spread with butter and jelly. Serves 4 to 6.

Vesta Geis
Vidor

Bea's Mexican Cornbread

1 cup cornmeal
2 tablespoons flour
2 tablespoons sugar
1 teaspoon salt
½ teaspoon baking soda
1 cup buttermilk
2 eggs
1 can cream-style corn
¼ cup bacon grease
1 medium onion, chopped
2 to 3 jalapeño peppers, chopped
1 cup grated Longhorn cheese

Mix together dry ingredients. Add all remaining ingredients except cheese. Pour half the mixture into a heavy iron skillet that has been greased and heated. Sprinkle with cheese and cover with remaining batter. Bake at 350 degrees for 1 hour.

Bea Cross
Dallas

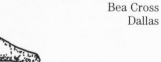

This recipe helped our family through the trying days of the Depression, when families made do, or substituted one thing for another. My Grand-daddy Cochran had this recipe for cornmeal dumplings. He would cut as much meat off the bone as he could, then the meat remaining was boiled on the bone for broth.

Cochran Cornmeal Dumplings

1 cup cornmeal
1 cup flour
1 teaspoon baking powder
½ teaspoon salt
¾ cup milk
1 egg, beaten
3 tablespoons shortening

Sift together cornmeal, flour, baking powder, and salt. Add milk, egg, and shortening and mix lightly. Drop into hot liquid by table-spoonfuls. Cover and cook 15 minutes without lifting lid.

Jean Fourmentin
Wellington

Leona Allcorn's "Grated" Cornbread

3 or 4 ears of corn
½ cup stone-ground yellow cornmeal
½ cup flour
2 teaspoons baking powder
½ teaspoon baking soda
1 teaspoon salt
2 tablespoons sugar
2 eggs, slightly beaten
3 tablespoons corn oil, divided
¾ to 1 cup buttermilk

Cut corn from cob, then scrape cob with back of knife to obtain juice. Puree slightly in a blender or food processor. Combine all dry ingredients and add pureed corn, eggs, 2 tablespoons oil, and buttermilk. Stir until well mixed, adding more milk if necessary. Batter should have the consistency of oatmeal. Spray an 8-inch round cast iron skillet or muffin tins with vegetable oil spray and add remaining 1 tablespoon oil. Heat in oven just until oil begins smoking. Spoon batter into skillet or muffin tins. Bake at 400 degrees for 25 to 30 minutes or until browned. (Muffins take less time.) Cut into wedges and serve immediately with butter. This cornbread can be very successfully reheated in a microwave if wrapped in a paper towel. Note: For turn-of-the-century West Texas authenticity, grate corn on a tin can with holes punched in it; use home-churned butter or bacon grease instead of oil; and cook in a wood stove.

Susan and Sally Caldwell
Garland

Our grandparents, Seth and Leona Allcorn, reared their seven daughters and three grandchildren on a farm in West Texas in the early 1900s. When the corn became too mature to eat straight off the cob, Leona would grate it to make cornbread.

War Worker Rolls of 1944

1 cup milk, scalded
2 tablespoons shortening
2 tablespoons sugar
1 cake compressed yeast
1 cup warm water
1 teaspoon salt
3 cups flour

Blend milk, shortening, and sugar and set aside to cool. Dissolve yeast and salt in warm water. Combine milk mixture and yeast mixture and add flour, blending thoroughly. Let rise 50 minutes. Make into rolls and place in greased pan; let rise 20 minutes. Bake at 350 degrees for 20 to 25 minutes.

Helen Collard
Arlington

Trail Driver's Sourdough Bread

SOURDOUGH STARTER
1 package dry yeast
1 quart lukewarm water
2 tablespoons sugar
4 cups sifted flour

BREAD
1 cup milk
⅓ cup shortening
⅓ cup sugar
1 teaspoon salt
1 package dry yeast or 1 cake compressed yeast
2 tablespoons lukewarm water
pinch of sugar
1½ cups sourdough starter
5 cups flour

To make starter, mix yeast and lukewarm water in a 3-quart crock. Add sugar and flour and beat well. Cover and let rise 24 to 28 hours or until light and slightly aged. Starter can be kept in the refrigerator seven to ten days without attention. Then it should be stirred and equal amounts of flour and water added. To use starter, pour off amount needed for recipe, then add flour and water to remaining starter.

To make bread, scald milk; then add shortening, sugar, and salt, stirring well. Cool until lukewarm. Dissolve yeast in lukewarm water with pinch of sugar. Beat together cooled milk mixture, dissolved yeast, starter, and 2 cups flour. Add remaining flour to make a stiff dough. Turn onto a floured surface and knead 5 to 10 minutes; add only enough flour to keep dough from sticking to surface. Place in greased bowl, turning to grease surface. Let rise 1½ to 2 hours or until doubled. Punch down and let rise again about 1½ hours. Divide into balls, cover with a towel, and let rest about 10 or 15 minutes. Shape into two loaves and place in two greased 9″ × 5″ × 3″ pans. Let rise 1 hour or until double. Bake at 400 degrees for about 40 minutes. Cool before slicing.

Martha A. Stahl
Bulverde

Yeast Rolls

1 cup milk
¼ cup butter
½ cup sugar
1 teaspoon salt
2 packages dry yeast
¼ cup lukewarm water
2 eggs, well beaten
4½ cups sifted flour

In a saucepan, heat milk, butter, sugar, and salt until butter melts. Do not boil. Dissolve yeast in warm water and add to milk mixture. Add eggs and flour. Stir in 2 cups flour and mix well, then gradually add remaining flour, kneading well. Form dough into a ball and place in a greased bowl. Let the dough rise until doubled. Punch down and pinch off pieces; arrange on greased cookie sheet or in muffin tins. Let rise until light. Bake at 375 degrees for approximately 30 minutes. Makes about 24 rolls. This recipe can also be used for cinnamon rolls and doughnuts.

Kathy Collins
Hillsboro

60-Minute Yeast Rolls

3½ to 4½ cups flour
3 tablespoons sugar
1 teaspoon salt
2 packages dry yeast
1 cup milk
½ cup water
¼ cup margarine

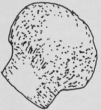

In a large bowl mix 1½ cups flour, sugar, salt, and yeast. In a saucepan, combine milk, water, and margarine. Heat over low heat until warm, but do not melt margarine. Add dry ingredients and beat 2 minutes at low speed on electric mixer. Add ½ cup flour. Beat at high speed for 2 minutes. Stir in enough flour to make soft dough. Turn out on a floured board and knead about 5 minutes. Place in a greased bowl, cover, and set bowl in a pan of warm water. Let rise 15 minutes. Turn out onto a floured board and divide in half. Pinch 12 portions from each half. Put in two greased muffin pans. Let rise 15 minutes in a warm place. Bake at 425 degrees for 12 minutes. Makes 24 rolls.

Dottie Morris
Fort Worth

Whole Wheat Rolls

3½ cups sifted whole wheat flour
2 packages dry yeast
2 cups milk
½ cup sugar
1 tablespoon salt
3 tablespoons shortening
2 eggs
3¼ to 3½ cups sifted all-purpose flour

In a large mixer bowl, combine whole wheat flour and yeast. In a saucepan, combine milk, sugar, salt, and shortening and heat just until warm, stirring occasionally to melt shortening. Add to dry ingredients. Add eggs. Beat at low speed with electric mixer for 30 seconds, scraping sides of bowl constantly. Beat 3 minutes at high speed. Stir in enough all-purpose flour to make a soft dough. Turn out onto a lightly floured surface and knead until smooth. Place in a greased bowl, turning over once to grease surface. Cover and let rise about 1½ hours or until double. Punch down, then cover and let rest 10 minutes. Shape into 24 rolls and place on greased baking sheets. Cover and let rise about 45 minutes or until almost double. Bake at 400 degrees for 15 to 20 minutes or until brown. Makes 24 rolls.

Patsy M. White
The Woodlands

This recipe came from a cookbook that our family put together with over 400 of our favorite recipes. It was dedicated to Carrie Saculla, who was known for her unforgettable bread and rolls. The Saculla family came to America via Louisiana and later migrated to the Brazos River bottoms in the late 1800s.

Carrie's Bread

6 cups very warm water
4 packages dry yeast or ⅓ to ½ cup fresh yeast
6 tablespoons vegetable oil
2 tablespoons sugar
2 tablespoons salt
1 5-pound bag flour

In a 10- to 12-quart bowl combine water and yeast and whisk until dissolved. Then add oil, sugar, and salt. Whisk together well and add half the bag of flour, continuing to mix well. Add remaining flour. Using your hands, work flour into batter until well mixed. Knead for 10 minutes or until dough is smooth. Knead dough on lightly floured board and place in well-greased bowl, turning dough over to grease top. Wrap in warm towels (or blankets or tablecloths). Let rise until doubled. To make loaves, punch down, knead, and divide in eight portions. Roll out each portion, one at a time, and spread with butter. Roll up and place in a well-greased loaf pan to rise until tripled. Allow plenty of room in pans. To make rolls, let rise again until almost doubled. Pinch off or cut off uniform pieces of dough and place in well-greased muffin tins. Let rise until tripled. Bake at 450 degrees until crusted and golden brown. Brush with margarine when starting to brown.

Marjorie Saculla
Bryan

Ethelyn's French Pancake

½ cup milk
½ cup flour
2 eggs, slightly beaten
⅛ teaspoon salt
¼ teaspoon nutmeg
8 tablespoons margarine
powdered sugar

Combine milk, flour, eggs, salt, and nutmeg and mix quickly (a few lumps are okay). Melt margarine in a 6-quart saucepan (with ovenproof handle) and heat until sizzling but not brown. Add batter quickly and bake at 425 degrees for 15 or 20 minutes or until the pancake puffs up. During the last 5 minutes of cooking time, sprinkle with powdered sugar. Cut in wedges and serve plain or with jam.

Ethelyn Conrad
Castroville

Tropical Banana Bread

1 cup butter or margarine
2 cups sugar
4 eggs
2 teaspoons vanilla
6 ripe bananas, mashed
1 8-ounce can crushed pineapple, drained
4 cups flour
2 teaspoons baking soda
1 teaspoon salt
1 cup chopped pecans

Cream together butter, sugar, eggs, and vanilla. Stir in bananas and pineapple. Add flour, baking soda, and salt and mix just until moistened. Stir in nuts. Pour batter into two greased and floured loaf pans. Bake at 325 degrees for 1 hour.

Gwen L. Hoyt
Kyle

Rosie Hithe's Cowboy Bread

2½ cups sifted all-purpose flour
2 cups brown sugar
½ teaspoon salt
¾ cup butter
2 teaspoons baking powder
½ teaspoon cinnamon
½ teaspoon nutmeg
½ teaspoon baking soda
1 cup sour milk
2 eggs, well beaten

Cut flour, brown sugar, and salt into butter until mixture has the consistency of fine crumbs. Set aside ½ cup; to remaining mixture add baking powder, cinnamon, and nutmeg and blend well. In a separate bowl dissolve soda in milk and add eggs. Beat well and pour into dry mixture, stirring until smooth. Pour into sheet pan to a depth of about 1 inch. Bake at 375 degrees for 30 minutes. Cut into squares and serve hot with coffee.

John Sparger
Dallas

Grandpa's B'wanga Bread

2 large, very ripe bananas, mashed
1 whole egg plus 1 egg white or 2 eggs
¼ cup milk (optional)
¼ cup sunflower oil
½ cup brown sugar
¼ cup white sugar
1 cup unbleached or all-purpose flour
½ cup whole wheat flour
½ cup oats
3 teaspoons double-acting baking powder
2 tablespoons brewer's yeast (optional)
2 tablespoons wheat germ (optional)
¼ cup nonfat dry milk (optional)
¼ cup sesame seeds (optional)
¼ cup raisins (optional)
½ cup nuts, chopped or whole

Mix bananas, eggs, and milk and set aside. In a medium bowl cream together oil and sugar, then add banana mixture and mix thoroughly. In a large bowl combine all remaining ingredients except raisins and nuts. Add banana mixture to the dry ingredients, then add nuts and raisins. Transfer batter to an oiled and floured loaf pan. Bake at 425 degrees for 15 minutes, reduce heat to 350 degrees, and continue baking for about 40 minutes or until a fork stuck into the center of the loaf comes out clean. Serve warm.

Jim Jeffries
Crockett

The best thing about this recipe is that you can vary the ingredients to fit what you have on hand—just maintain the balance between dry and wet ingredients. We devised this recipe for our eldest grandson, who wasn't much of an eater. The one thing he liked was bananas—he just couldn't quite get the word right.

Jim Jeffries has been carving wooden carousel horses for the past twenty years.

Saddlebag Chew Bread

1 16-ounce package light brown sugar
4 eggs
2 cups all-purpose flour
½ teaspoon salt
1 teaspoon vanilla
1 cup chopped nuts, optional

In a heavy saucepan combine sugar and eggs, stirring well. Cook over medium heat until sugar dissolves, stirring constantly. Remove from heat and add remaining ingredients, stirring well. Spoon mixture into well-greased and floured 15″ × 10″ × 1″ jelly-roll pan. Bake at 400 degrees for 10 to 15 minutes or until golden brown. Cool and cut into squares. Makes about 3 dozen.

Mrs. D. E. Newberry
Lexington

Cornmeal Pancakes

4 teaspoons baking powder
1 cup flour
1 cup yellow cornmeal
1 teaspoon salt
1¾ cups milk
2 eggs, beaten
2 tablespoons butter, melted

Mix dry ingredients. In a separate bowl combine milk and melted butter and add beaten eggs. Combine the wet and dry mixtures. Bake over medium-high heat about 1 minute on each side. Makes 15 pancakes.

Carmen L. Martinez
San Antonio

This was a runner-up in the 1987 Burleson County Kolache Festival in Caldwell. Kolaches are a Czech pastry that is traditionally served at large celebrations such as weddings. They can be filled with prunes, peaches, poppyseeds, apricots, or even sausage.

Kolaches

½ cup sugar
½ cup butter or margarine
1 teaspoon salt
½ cup boiling water
1½ packages dry yeast
½ cup warm water
1 egg, beaten
3 to 3½ cups flour
melted butter or margarine

Cream together sugar, butter, and salt. Add boiling water and stir well. Let cool until lukewarm. Add yeast to warm water and let stand until dissolved, then add beaten egg. Combine the two mixtures, add flour, and mix well. Let rise about 30 minutes or until doubled. Roll out dough to a thickness of about ½ inch and cut into individual kolaches with a biscuit cutter. Place kolaches on a greased pan so they are not quite touching. Brush tops with melted butter, cover, and let rise again until light. Make an indention in the top of each and fill with the filling of your choice. Bake at 350 degrees about 25 minutes or until brown. Brush tops again with melted butter.

Dorothy Kubena
Caldwell

Delicious Nut Bread

2 cups instant oatmeal
1 cup All-Bran
2½ cups flour
2 rounded teaspoons Rumford baking powder
1½ level teaspoons baking soda
2 rounded teaspoons cinnamon
7 packets Sweet and Low
½ cup chopped nuts
2 large bananas, mashed
1 10-ounce jar Polaner All-Fruit strawberry jam
2 teaspoons vanilla
3 egg whites
¾ cup buttermilk
1 cup chopped apples

In a large bowl mix oatmeal, All-Bran, flour, baking powder, soda, cinnamon, Sweet and Low, and nuts in a large bowl. In a separate bowl mix remaining ingredients. Combine banana mixture with oatmeal mixture and mix just enough to blend all ingredients together; batter should be thick. Pour into a 9″ × 13″ oblong pan that has been lightly oiled (or spoon into muffin tins). Bake at 350 degrees for 35 to 40 minutes or until done.

Pauline Martin
Brazoria

T his nut bread is sugar free, fat free, and cholesterol free.

Dark Zucchini Bread

3 large eggs, beaten
2 cups sugar
1 cup oil
1 tablespoon vanilla
2 cups flour
3 tablespoons cinnamon
2 teaspoons baking soda
¼ teaspoon baking powder
1 teaspoon salt
2 cups grated zucchini
1½ cups chopped pecans

Combine eggs and sugar and beat well. Mix in oil and vanilla. Sift together flour, cinnamon, soda, baking powder, and salt and add to egg and sugar mixture. Stir in zucchini and pecans. Pour into two greased and floured 9″ × 5″ bread pans. Bake at 350 degrees for 1 hour.

Elizabeth J. Sigmon
Stephenville

My grandmother taught me how to make this prize-winning gingerbread when I was about ten years old. It was one of the first things I learned to cook.

Barbara and Zack Payton are the owners of the Starbrite Tree Farm in Lubbock, where people can cut their own Christmas trees during the holiday season.

Blue Ribbon Gingerbread

½ cup butter
½ cup sugar
1 egg, beaten
1 cup molasses
2½ cups flour
1½ teaspoons baking soda
1 teaspoon cinnamon
1 teaspoon ginger
½ teaspoon cloves
½ teaspoon allspice
½ teaspoon salt
1 cup hot water

Cream together butter and sugar. Add egg and molasses. Sift dry ingredients together and add to creamed mixture. Add hot water, mix quickly, and pour into shallow pan. Bake at 350 degrees for 45 minutes.

Barbara Payton
Lubbock

Gingerbread

½ cup butter
½ cup sugar
1 cup molasses
½ teaspoon baking soda
1 cup boiling water
2½ cups sifted flour
1 teaspoon cloves
1 teaspoon cinnamon
1 teaspoon ginger
½ teaspoon salt
2 eggs, beaten

Cream together butter and sugar. Add molasses and baking soda dissolved in boiling water. Sift together flour, spices, and salt and add to butter and molasses mixture. Add beaten eggs. Bake in greased pan at 350 degrees for 20 minutes.

Jeanie Smith Atwell
Dallas

Apple Muffins

2 cups flour
½ cup sugar
1 tablespoon baking powder
¼ teaspoon salt
1 cup chopped apples
1 egg, beaten
1 cup milk
3 tablespoons butter, melted

TOPPING
⅓ cup brown sugar
½ teaspoon cinnamon
⅓ cup chopped pecans

Stir together flour, sugar, baking powder, and salt. In a separate bowl combine remaining ingredients. Mix wet ingredients into dry ingredients and stir just enough to moisten. Spoon into a buttered muffin tin, filling only half full. Mix topping ingredients together and sprinkle over batter. Bake at 400 degrees for 15 minutes. Makes 12 muffins.

Sylvia Thompson
Tyler

Orange Muffins

1 cup margarine
1 cup sugar
2 eggs
2 cups flour
1 teaspoon baking soda
¾ cup buttermilk
1 teaspoon lemon extract
2 tablespoons fine-grated orange rind
1 cup dates
¼ cup orange juice

GLAZE
1 cup orange juice
2 cups sugar

Cream together margarine and sugar. Add eggs and beat well. Add flour and soda alternately with buttermilk. Add remaining ingredients. Spoon into greased miniature muffin tins and bake at 400 degrees for 12 minutes. To make glaze, mix orange juice and sugar, bring to a boil, remove from heat, and cool. Dip warm muffins into glaze and cool on wax paper. Makes approximately 150 miniature muffins. These muffins can be frozen for a few days and are great for brunches.

Gen Hellums
Freer

DESSERTS

CAKES

Fresh Rome Apple Cake, Texas Style

1½ cups corn oil
2 cups sugar
3 eggs
3 cups flour
1 teaspoon baking powder
½ teaspoon baking soda
1 teaspoon cinnamon
1 teaspoon nutmeg
1 teaspoon salt
1 teaspoon vanilla
3 Rome apples, cored and grated
1 cup chopped nuts

Mix all ingredients together, stirring well. Bake at 325 degrees for 1½ hours in tube pan or Bundt pan.

June G. Pryor
Texarkana

Applesauce Cake

2 cups flour
1 teaspoon baking powder
2 teaspoons baking soda
½ teaspoon cloves
½ teaspoon nutmeg
½ teaspoon salt
1 teaspoon cinnamon
½ cup shortening
1 cup brown sugar, firmly packed
1 cup chopped raisins
½ cup chopped pecans
1 can unsweetened applesauce

ICING
1 stick margarine
1 box powdered sugar
1 teaspoon vanilla
milk

Sift together flour, baking powder, soda, cloves, nutmeg, salt, and cinnamon. In a separate bowl cream shortening and brown sugar. Add raisins, pecans, and applesauce. Add to dry ingredients and mix well. Bake in a greased 9″ × 13″ pan at 350 degrees for 30 minutes or until a toothpick inserted in center comes out clean. Cool. To make icing, cream together margarine, powdered sugar, vanilla, and enough milk to give mixture the consistency for spreading. Spread icing on cooled cake. Note: This recipe can also be used for cupcakes, but the baking time should be adjusted.

Sue O. Byers
Dallas

Banana Cake

⅔ cup shortening or oil
1⅔ cups sugar
2 egg yolks plus 1 whole egg
1¼ cups mashed bananas
2½ cups sifted flour
1¼ teaspoons baking powder
1 teaspoon salt
1 teaspoon baking soda
⅔ cup buttermilk

FROSTING
1 pint whipping cream
2 egg whites
1 tablespoon vanilla
¾ cup powdered sugar
bananas, sliced

This is our family's favorite birthday cake.

Stir shortening until softened, then cream together with sugar. Add eggs and mix well. Stir in bananas. In a separate bowl sift together all dry ingredients. Slowly add dry ingredients to shortening mixture, alternating with buttermilk. Beat vigorously for 2 minutes. Bake in wax-paper-lined cake pans at 350 degrees for about 35 minutes. Cool 10 minutes before removing from pan. To make frosting, beat whipping cream and egg whites until stiff peaks form. While still beating, add vanilla and powdered sugar. Continue to beat until mixed well, but before butter begins to form. Sprinkle banana slices over top of first layer, then top with frosting. Cover with second layer, sprinkle with bananas, and top with frosting. Cover sides of cake with frosting. Refrigerate until ready to serve.

Mrs. R. M. Parks
Dallas

Coriander Cake

1 package yellow cake mix
1 package instant vanilla pudding mix
3 eggs
1 cup vegetable oil
1 teaspoon coriander
1 teaspoon cinnamon
2 small jars apricot baby food
1 cup chopped pecans

GLAZE
juice of 1 lemon
⅓ cup sugar
½ stick margarine

Mix all ingredients together and pour into a greased and floured tube or Bundt pan. Bake at 325 degrees for 50 to 60 minutes. To make glaze, mix together lemon juice, sugar, and margarine and bring to a boil. Punch holes in cake and pour glaze over warm cake.

Yvonne Ross
Longview

Aunt Elsie's Carrot Cake

For a long time my children and I thought this was the only kind of carrot cake there was. You can imagine our surprise when we finally decided to order carrot cake in a restaurant and it did not have cocoa in it.

2 cups flour
2 cups sugar
2 teaspoons baking soda
1 teaspoon salt
½ cup cocoa
4 eggs
1 teaspoon vanilla
1½ cups vegetable oil
2 cups grated carrots
1 cup crushed pineapple, undrained

ICING
1 8-ounce package cream cheese
1 stick butter
1 box powdered sugar
½ cup coconut
1 cup chopped nuts

Combine dry ingredients. In a separate bowl mix together eggs, vanilla, and oil and add to dry ingredients, mixing well. Stir in carrots and crushed pineapple. Pour into three 9-inch round greased cake pans and bake at 350 degrees for 30 minutes or until toothpick inserted in center comes out clean. Cool before icing. To make icing, combine cream cheese, butter, and powdered sugar and beat well. Fold in coconut and nuts. Spread on cooled cake. Refrigerate until ready to serve.

Helen Kalmes
Cibolo

Christmas Fruit Cake

1 cup applesauce, heated
2 teaspoons baking soda
1 cup sugar
¾ cup shortening
1 teaspoon salt
1 teaspoon cinnamon
1 teaspoon cloves
1 teaspoon nutmeg
3 eggs
½ pound pecans, chopped
2 7½-ounce packages dates
½ pound candied cherries
1 small jar peach preserves
½ small jar pineapple preserves
3 cups flour

This is an original recipe from my mother, Ada Bane. The rest of the family didn't like fruit cake, so through trial and error she came up with one we liked very much.

Mix applesauce and baking soda. Cream together shortening and sugar and mix with applesauce. Add remaining ingredients in order listed. Pour into a greased and floured tube pan and place on oven rack over a pan of water. Bake at 300 degrees for 2 hours or until done.

Mrs. Floyd Verheyden
Jacksonville

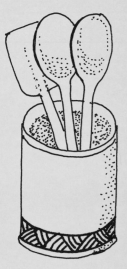

Red Velvet Cake

3 tablespoons cocoa
1 ounce red food coloring
1 ounce water
½ cup shortening
1½ cups sugar
2 eggs, beaten
2¼ cups flour
1 teaspoon salt
1 cup buttermilk
1 teaspoon vanilla
1 tablespoon vinegar
1 teaspoon baking soda

"WHIPPED CREAM" FROSTING
1 stick margarine
½ cup shortening
1 cup powdered sugar
3 tablespoons flour
⅔ cup milk at room temperature
1 teaspoon vanilla

Mix cocoa, food coloring, and water and set aside. Cream together shortening and sugar. Add eggs and cocoa paste and beat at least 15 minutes. Add flour and salt alternately with buttermilk. Add vanilla. Mix vinegar and baking soda, then stir into batter. Pour into two greased and floured 9-inch-round pans or one 9″ × 13″ pan. Bake at 350 degrees for 30 to 35 minutes (round pans) or 35 to 40 minutes (oblong pan). Cool before frosting. To make frosting, cream together margarine, shortening, and powdered sugar. Add flour 1 tablespoon at a time, mixing well after each addition. Add milk and vanilla. Beat until mixture is the texture of whipped cream. Spread over cooled cake.

Sue C. Hall
Bellaire

One-Hundred-Dollar Chocolate Cake

2 cups flour
2 teaspoons baking powder
½ cup margarine
2 cups sugar
2 eggs, beaten
4 squares chocolate, melted
1½ cups milk
2 teaspoons vanilla
½ cup nuts

ICING
¼ pound margarine
1 egg, beaten
1 teaspoon vanilla
1 cup chopped pecans
2 squares chocolate
¾ box powdered sugar

Sift together flour and baking powder and set aside. Cream together margarine and sugar. Add eggs and chocolate. Add milk and dry ingredients alternately. Beat well and add vanilla and nuts. Bake in two 9-inch round pans at 350 degrees for 30 minutes. Cool before icing. To make icing, melt margarine and chocolate together and cool. Add egg. Gradually add powdered sugar, mixing well after each addition. Add vanilla and nuts.

Sharon Rogers
Memphis

Cocoa Chocolate Cake

2 cups flour
1 teaspoon baking powder
¾ teaspoon salt
1 teaspoon baking soda
½ cup cocoa
1½ cups sugar
½ cup shortening
½ cup water
1 teaspoon vanilla
¼ teaspoon almond extract (optional)
3 eggs
¾ cup buttermilk

Jim Ella Simpson is a professional baker whose specialties are wedding cakes and gingerbread houses.

In a mixer bowl combine all ingredients except buttermilk and mix 2 minutes using an electric mixer. Add buttermilk in thirds, then mix 1 minute. Pour into two greased and floured 9-inch round cake pans or one 9″ × 13″ pan. Bake at 350 degrees for 30 to 35 minutes.

Jim Ella Simpson
Post

Y ou have to be a
"chocoholic" to really
like this cake. It is the
very best chocolate cake
I've ever tasted—just
like Grandma used to
make.

Mexica Chocolate Cake

1 cup water
1 stick margarine
4 tablespoons cocoa
½ cup shortening
2 cups flour
2 cups sugar
1 teaspoon cinnamon
1 teaspoon baking soda
½ cup buttermilk
2 eggs
1 teaspoon vanilla

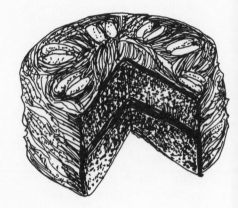

ICING
1 stick margarine
4 tablespoons cocoa
6 tablespoons milk
1 box powdered sugar
1 teaspoon vanilla
1 cup pecans

In a saucepan mix together water, margarine, cocoa, and short-ening; melt and bring to a boil. Add remaining ingredients and mix well. Pour into a greased oblong pan and bake at 400 degrees for about 20 minutes. To make icing, combine margarine, cocoa, and milk and heat until margarine melts. Add sugar and vanilla. Beat well. Add pecans. Spread on cake.

Betty Dunn
Euless

Better-Than-Sex Cake

1 package yellow cake mix
1 15-ounce can crushed pineapple, undrained

ICING
1 8-ounce package cream cheese
1 8-ounce container La Creme or Cool Whip
1 3½-ounce package vanilla instant pudding

Prepare mix according to directions on package and bake in a 9″ × 13″ pan. While warm, spread with pineapple. Blend together cream cheese, La Creme, and pudding. Spread over cake and refrigerate.

Carole A. Elrod
Dallas

Mississippi Mud Cake

1 cup margarine, melted
2 cups sugar
4 eggs
1 teaspoon vanilla
1½ cups flour
2 tablespoons cocoa
1½ cups chopped pecans
1 can coconut
1 7-ounce jar marshmallow cream

ICING
1 box powdered sugar
½ cup margarine, melted
½ cup evaporated milk
⅓ cup cocoa
1 teaspoon vanilla

Mix together all ingredients except marshmallow cream. Pour into a greased and floured 9″ × 13″ pan and bake at 350 degrees for 35 minutes. Remove from oven and cool slightly. Punch holes in top of cake with knitting needle or ice pick and spread warm cake with marshmallow cream. Set aside to cool. To make icing, mix together all ingredients. Pour over cooled cake.

Mrs. Hershel R. Phillips
Farmersville

I have been decorating cakes professionally for well over thirty years. The wedding cakes I have made number in the hundreds. During that time this is the only chocolate cake recipe I have used for birthday cakes and groom cakes.

Vinegar and Air Cake

4 eggs, separated
1 teaspoon vinegar
1 cup sugar
1 cup cake flour, sifted twice
1 teaspoon vanilla

Beat egg yolks until light and fluffy; add vinegar. Beat egg whites until stiff but not dry. Add yolks to whites. Add sugar gradually, then add flour gradually. Stir in vanilla. Pour in a greased and floured 9″ × 13″ pan and bake at 375 degrees for 35 minutes. Cut into squares and top with fresh strawberries.

Mary Walters Allen
Camp Verde

Black Walnut Cake

1 cup butter, softened
½ cup shortening
2 cups light brown sugar, packed
1 cup granulated sugar
5 eggs
3 cups flour
½ teaspoon baking powder
¼ teaspoon salt
1 cup milk
1 tablespoon vanilla
1 cup fine-chopped black walnuts

FROSTING
¼ cup butter, softened
1 3-ounce package cream cheese, softened
2 to 3 tablespoons milk

Cream butter and shortening. Gradually add sugars, beating well at medium speed. Add eggs one at a time, beating well after each addition. In a separate bowl combine flour, salt, and baking powder. Add to the butter mixture alternately with milk, beginning and ending with the flour mixture. Stir in vanilla and walnuts. Pour batter into a greased and floured tube pan. Bake at 325 degrees for 1 hour and 30 minutes. Cool. To make frosting, cream together ingredients and beat until smooth. Spread over cooled cake.

Ruby Turner
Willis

We've had a lot of laughs about this "sad" cake. It really does look sad, but it's delicious.

Sad Cake

4 eggs, slightly beaten
1 package brown sugar
2 cups Bisquick
1 cup coconut
1 cup pecans
2 teaspoons vanilla

Mix all ingredients together and pour into a greased 9″ × 13″ pan. Bake at 350 degrees for 20 to 25 minutes or until golden brown.

Evelyn Morris
Moody

Depression Cake

1 cup shortening
2 cups water
2 cups raisins
1 teaspoon cinnamon
1 teaspoon nutmeg
1 teaspoon allspice
½ teaspoon cloves
2 cups sugar
3 cups flour
1 teaspoon baking soda

In a kettle combine all ingredients except flour and soda and simmer for 10 minutes. Remove from heat and let stand until cool. Add flour and soda and pour into a 9″ × 13″ greased pan. Bake at 350 degrees for 45 minutes.

Doris Baber
Fritch

This was called Depression Cake because it contains no eggs, butter, or milk. My mother baked it in the early thirties and passed the recipe on to me. Now my daughters and granddaughters also use it.

Pineapple Nut Cake

2 cups flour
2 cups sugar
2 eggs
2 teaspoons baking soda
½ teaspoon salt
1 cup chopped nuts
1 20-ounce can crushed pineapple, undrained

FROSTING
1 8-ounce package cream cheese
1 stick margarine
2 tablespoons milk
2 cups powdered sugar
1 teaspoon vanilla extract

Mix all ingredients together well. Pour into a greased and floured 9″ × 13″ pan. Bake at 350 degrees for 35 to 40 minutes. To make frosting, mix all ingredients together until smooth and creamy. Spread over slightly warm cake.

N. Dolores Willis
Jasper

Oatmeal Cake

1¼ cups boiling water
1 cup oats
1 stick margarine
1 cup white sugar
1 cup brown sugar
2 eggs
1½ cups flour
1 teaspoon baking soda
½ teaspoon cinnamon
¼ teaspoon salt

ICING
1 cup chopped nuts
1 cup coconut
½ cup sugar
¼ cup cream
6 tablespoons margarine
2 teaspoons vanilla

Pour boiling water over oats and margarine. Let stand 20 minutes. (If using quick oats, let stand 5 minutes.) Add remaining ingredients and beat well. Pour into a 9″ × 13″ greased and floured pan. Bake at 300 degrees for about 45 minutes. To make icing, combine all ingredients and spread over warm cake. Place under the broiler until brown (watch closely to make sure it does not burn).

Betty Whitehead
Port Neches

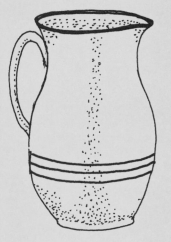

When I first compiled my collection of recipes in the early 1930s, this cake became a Christmas necessity. At that time 2 ounces of lemon extract was 25 cents. This last year I paid $1.69 for the same. How times have changed! But not my Christmas cake.

Pecan Cake

¾ pound butter or margarine
3 cups sugar
6 eggs, separated
2 ounces lemon extract
3 cups flour
1 quart pecans
1 pound raisins

Cream butter and sugar. Add egg yolks one at a time, mixing well after each addition. Add lemon extract. Add flour, nuts, and raisins. Beat egg whites and fold in, mixing well. Pour into a well-greased and floured tube pan and bake at 225 degrees for 3 hours or less.

Mary Elizabeth Grimes
Dallas

Hard Times Cake

1 cup raisins
2 cups cold water
1 teaspoon baking soda
2 cups all-purpose flour
1 cup granulated sugar
2 tablespoons lard or shortening
½ teaspoon salt
1 teaspoon cinnamon
1 teaspoon nutmeg

In a small saucepan combine raisins and water, bring to a boil, and boil for 5 minutes. Drain raisins and set aside. To 1 cup of the raisin water add baking soda and flour. In a separate bowl cream together sugar and lard, then add to flour mixture. Add salt and spices. Stir in reserved raisins. Pour batter into two small well-greased loaf pans. Bake at 350 degrees for 25 minutes or until cake tester inserted in center of cake comes out clean.

Mattie Bush
Dallas

Legend has it that this cake was devised before the turn of the century by a school-teacher who got snowed in and was faced with a dwindling supply of staples. The recipe has been passed down in my family for years—it's over one hundred years old now.

Funnel Cakes

1 egg, beaten
⅔ cup milk
2 tablespoons sugar
1⅓ cups sifted flour
¼ teaspoon salt
¾ teaspoon baking powder
vegetable oil
powdered sugar

Combine egg and milk and set aside. Sift sugar, flour, salt, and baking powder together; add egg and milk mixture. Beat until smooth. Heat oil to 375 degrees. Pour batter into funnel, keeping finger over spout. Hold funnel over hot oil, remove finger, and allow batter to drop into oil—about ¼ cup at a time. Make swirls from the center out. Deep-fry until golden brown, turning once. Drain. Sprinkle with powdered sugar and serve warm.

Shirley Embrey
San Antonio

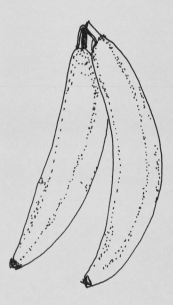

Hummingbird Cake

3 cups flour
2 cups sugar
¼ teaspoon salt
1 teaspoon cinnamon
3 eggs
1½ cups oil
1½ teaspoons vanilla
1 8-ounce can crushed pineapple, drained
2 cups mashed bananas
1½ cups chopped pecans

FROSTING
1 8-ounce package cream cheese
½ cup margarine
1 16-ounce box powdered sugar
1 teaspoon vanilla
½ cup chopped pecans

In a large bowl combine dry ingredients. Add eggs and oil, mixing well. Stir in vanilla, pineapple, bananas, and pecans. Spoon into three 9-inch round greased and floured pans. Bake at 350 degrees for 40 minutes or until done. Cool 10 minutes before removing from pans. To make frosting, combine all ingredients except pecans and mix well. Spread over cooled layers and sprinkle with pecans.

Mrs. Lloyd McCord
Clarendon

This cake recipe came from Paul Thompson, the cook for outfitter Max Wilde of Cody, Wyoming. He baked a one-layer prune cake in a wood stove in camp. This became our prize cake for special occasions such as birthdays.

Festive Prune Cake

2 cups flour
1 teaspoon baking soda
1 teaspoon salt
1 teaspoon cinnamon
¼ teaspoon nutmeg
¼ teaspoon cloves
¼ teaspoon allspice
½ cup shortening
1 cup sugar
2 eggs
1 cup prune juice
1 cup cooked chopped prunes
1 cup nuts

Sift together dry ingredients and set aside. Cream together shortening and sugar, then blend in eggs, one at a time. Beat 1 minute. Add dry ingredients alternately with prune juice, beginning and ending with the dry ingredients. Fold in prunes and nuts. Pour into a greased and floured 9″ × 13″ pan or two 8-inch round pans. Bake at 350 degrees for approximately 30 minutes or until cake tests done.

Mr. and Mrs. Jim Penton
Rosston

Sam Houston White Cake

¾ cup margarine or butter, softened
2 cups sugar
3 cups all-purpose flour
1 teaspoon baking powder
½ teaspoon salt
½ cup milk
½ cup water
1 teaspoon almond extract
6 egg whites at room temperature

FROSTING
3 1-ounce squares unsweetened chocolate
4 cups sifted powdered sugar
⅛ teaspoon salt
¼ cup hot water
3 egg yolks
¼ cup butter or margarine, melted
1 teaspoon vanilla extract

According to legend, this was Sam Houston's favorite cake recipe.

Cream butter and gradually add sugar, beating well. Combine flour, baking powder, and salt. Combine milk and water. Add flour mixture to butter mixture alternately with milk mixture, beginning and ending with flour mixture. Mix well after each addition. Stir in almond extract. Beat egg whites until stiff peaks form and fold into batter. Pour batter into three greased and floured 9-inch round cake pans. Bake at 350 degrees for 25 minutes. Cool before frosting. To make frosting, melt chocolate in top of double boiler over boiling water. Remove from heat. Add powdered sugar, salt, and hot water. Beat on medium speed of electric mixer until thoroughly blended. Add egg yolks one at a time, stirring well after each addition. Add butter and vanilla, beating until frosting reaches spreading consistency.

Diana M. Weise
Yorktown

The name means
Lightning Cake—
because it's so fast
and easy!

Jeanette Klein is a park
ranger at the LBJ State
Historical Park in Stone-
wall, which operates the
Sauer-Beckman Living
History Farmstead. The
homestead goes back
one hundred years and
illustrates many fea-
tures of German Hill
Country pioneer life.

Lottie Lee's Irish Potato Cake

1 cup butter or margarine
1½ cups sugar
3 eggs
1 cup mashed Irish potatoes at room temperature
1 cup buttermilk
2 cups sifted flour
2 teaspoons baking powder
½ teaspoon cinnamon
¼ teaspoon allspice
1 teaspoon vanilla
1 cup chopped pecans

ICING
2 cups sugar
1 teaspoon vanilla
2 sticks butter or margarine
½ cup milk

Cream butter and sugar, add eggs, and mix well. Add potatoes
and buttermilk. In a separate bowl mix dry ingredients, then add
to potato mixture. Mix well. Pour into three greased and floured
9-inch cake pans and bake at 350 degrees until done. To make
icing, combine ingredients and cook over medium heat until it
forms a soft ball in cold water. Remove from heat, cool, and beat
until thick enough to spread.

Lee Ona Swofford Lyles
Ponder

Blitz Kuchen

1 cup butter
1 cup sugar
4 eggs, beaten
1 cup flour
1 teaspoon baking powder
1 teaspoon vanilla

Cream together butter and sugar. Add eggs and mix well. In a
separate bowl sift together flour and baking powder. Add to butter mixture along with vanilla and mix well. Spread in a buttered
pan and bake at 350 degrees for about 25 minutes. Serve with a
powdered sugar icing or with whipped cream topping.

Jeanette Klein
Stonewall

Old-Fashioned Pineapple Upside-Down Cake

1 large can sliced pineapple
¼ cup margarine
⅔ cup light brown sugar, packed
⅓ cup chopped pecans
¼ cup chopped maraschino cherries
1 cup all-purpose flour
¾ cup granulated sugar
1½ teaspoons baking powder
½ teaspoon salt
¼ cup shortening
½ cup milk
1 egg

Drain pineapple, reserving 2 tablespoons of the syrup. In a 10-inch cast iron skillet, melt margarine over medium heat. Add brown sugar, stirring until sugar is melted. Remove from heat; arrange pineapple slices on sugar mixture, overlapping slices slightly around edge of skillet. Sprinkle pecans and cherries on top of slices. In a medium bowl, sift flour with granulated sugar, baking powder, and salt. Add shortening and milk. With electric mixer at high speed, beat 2 minutes or until mixture is smooth. Add egg and reserved pineapple syrup. Beat 2 minutes longer. Gently pour into skillet, spreading evenly and being careful not to disturb pineapple slices. Place on rack in center of oven. Bake at 350 degrees 35 to 40 minutes until golden in color and surface of cake springs back when gently pressed with fingertip. Cool on wire rack 5 minutes. With small spatula, loosen cake from edge of skillet all around. Place serving platter over skillet and turn cake out gently. Let cool. Keep refrigerated.

Roger Dale and
Mary Kay Martin
Azle

This pineapple upside-down cake recipe was given to me by my mother-in-law, Mary Alice Chance Martin. She got it out of a *Better Homes and Gardens* cookbook in 1943. It's the best you'll ever eat! The flavor and texture of the sponge cake is the secret. It's not too sweet—it's just right.

Old-Fashioned Pound Cake

1 cup shortening
2 cups sugar
4 eggs
3 cups flour, sifted three times
1 cup buttermilk
½ teaspoon salt
½ teaspoon baking soda
1 teaspoon orange extract
1 teaspoon lemon extract

Iness Arey is a painter who is often called another Grandma Moses.

In an electric mixer, cream together shortening and sugar. Add eggs, one at a time, and beat well. Add flour alternately with buttermilk. Add remaining ingredients. Pour into a greased tube pan and bake at 325 degrees for 1 hour or more.

Iness Arey
Garland

Cream Cheese Pound Cake

1 cup margarine, softened
½ cup butter, softened
1 8-ounce package cream cheese, softened
3 cups sugar
dash of salt
2 teaspoons vanilla
6 large eggs
3 cups flour

Combine margarine, butter, cream cheese, and sugar. Mix well. Add salt and vanilla, then add eggs one at a time, beating well after each addition. Add flour and mix well. Pour into a greased and floured 10-inch tube pan. Place in cold oven and set temperature at 275 degrees. Bake 1½ hours or until done. Cool in pan. Glaze with favorite glaze if desired.

Jeannette Lee
Caddo Mills

Coca Cola Cake

2 cups unsifted flour
2 cups sugar
2 sticks margarine
3 tablespoons cocoa
1 cup Coca Cola
½ cup buttermilk
2 beaten eggs
1 teaspoon baking soda
1 teaspoon vanilla
½ cup miniature marshmallows

ICING
½ cup margarine
3 tablespoons cocoa
6 tablespoons Coca Cola
1 box powdered sugar
1 cup chopped pecans

Combine flour and sugar in a mixing bowl and set aside. Heat margarine, cocoa, and Coke to boiling and pour over flour and sugar mixture, mixing well. Add buttermilk, eggs, baking soda, and vanilla. Stir in marshmallows, which will float on top. Pour into a greased sheet cake pan and bake at 350 degrees for 30 to 35 minutes. Ice while warm. To make icing, combine margarine, cocoa, and Coke; heat to boiling. Pour over sugar and beat well. Add pecans. Spread over warm cake.

Shirley Wyche
Pampa

Scripture Cake

4½ cups flour (1 Kings 4:22)
1 cup butter (Judges 5:25)
2 cups sugar (Jeremiah 6:20)
2 cups raisins (1 Samuel 30:12)
2 cups figs (Nahum 3:12)
2 cups almonds (Numbers 17:8)
2 tablespoons honey (1 Samuel 14:25)
pinch of salt (Leviticus 2:13)
6 eggs (Jeremiah 17:11)
1¼ cups milk (Judges 4:19)
2 teaspoons baking soda (Amos 4:5)
spices to taste (2 Chronicles 9:9)

Mix all ingredients as for a fruit cake. Bake at 375 degrees for 1 hour. Spread with frosting or sprinkle with powdered sugar.

Arnold L. Rash
Silsbee

Arnold Rash was only sixteen years old when he began climbing telephone poles and installing glass telephone insulators. Known throughout Southeast Texas as "The Insulator Man," he has collected more than 4,000 glass insulators over the years.

My mother found this recipe on a coconut package when she was a young girl. It's still a family favorite.

Special Chocolate Icing

1½ cups sugar
1½ tablespoons cocoa
2 or 3 tablespoons butter or margarine
1½ tablespoons corn syrup
½ teaspoon vanilla extract
½ cup milk

Combine all ingredients and cook until mixture forms a soft ball in cold water.

Martha Faye Savage
Denton

Coconut Frosting

2 cups milk
1 cup granulated sugar
5 or 6 tablespoons flour
2 egg whites, beaten stiff
2 cups coconut

Scald milk but do not boil. Set aside. Add sugar and flour to egg whites, mixing well, then add milk. Cook until thick. Remove from heat and stir in coconut. Cool. Makes enough to frost a two-layer 8-inch cake.

LaNell Stancell
Muleshoe

PIES

Texas Praline-Apple Pie

2 pie crusts
5 to 6 baking apples, peeled, cored, and sliced
½ cup sugar
2 tablespoons flour
1 teaspoon cinnamon
¼ teaspoon nutmeg
1½ tablespoons lemon juice
butter

TOPPING
½ stick margarine or butter
½ cup brown sugar
2 tablespoons evaporated milk
½ cup chopped pecans
whipping cream

Line pie pan with bottom crust. Layer apples in crust and sprinkle with dry ingredients and lemon juice. Dot with butter and cover with top pie crust. Bake at 450 degrees for 10 minutes. Lower temperature to 350 degrees and bake 45 to 50 minutes or until done. To make topping, bring margarine, sugar, and milk to a boil over medium heat. Stir in pecans. Spread on top of baked pie. Serve with cinnamon-flavored whipping cream.

Cathy Godfrey
Bryan

Brazos Blackberry Pie

⅔ to 1 cup sugar
½ tablespoon cornstarch (or 3 to 4 tablespoons flour)
⅛ teaspoon salt
3 cups fresh blackberries
pie pastry
1 tablespoon butter or margarine

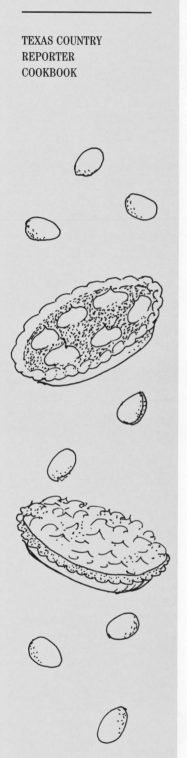

TOPPING
2 teaspoons sugar
1 teaspoon cinnamon

Combine sugar, cornstarch, and salt. Fold in berries. Fill pastry-lined pie pan with the mixture, dot with butter, and top with lattice strips of pastry. Sprinkle top of lattice crust with topping. Bake at 450 degrees for 10 minutes, then reduce heat to 350 degrees and bake for about 30 minutes.

Irene M. Hill
San Antonio

Chocolate Icebox Pie

1 cup sugar
4 tablespoons cocoa
4 tablespoons flour
2 eggs
1 cup milk
1 teaspoon vanilla
1 tablespoon butter
1 baked pie shell
1 8-ounce carton whipped topping

In a saucepan mix sugar, cocoa, and flour together. In a separate bowl beat eggs and milk together and add to cocoa mixture. Cook over medium heat until very thick (with the consistency of bread dough). Remove from heat; add vanilla and butter. With electric hand mixer, beat on the highest speed about 1 minute or until filling is smooth. Pour into baked pie shell. Chill, then cover with topping. Garnish with grated chocolate, if desired. (This recipe can be doubled for a fuller pie.)

Gay Bruton
Alice

Extra-Rich Chocolate Cream Pie

6 tablespoons flour
1½ cups sugar
3 tablespoons cocoa
1 large can evaporated milk
2 egg yolks, beaten
1 teaspoon vanilla
3 tablespoons margarine, melted
2 egg whites, beaten stiff
1 baked pie crust

Mix flour, sugar, and cocoa. Add milk, egg yolks, vanilla, and margarine. Cook in a double boiler until thick. Pour into baked pie crust. Top with meringue and bake for 15 minutes at 250 degrees.

Peggy M. Keen
Clifton

Hershey Bar Pie

2 8-ounce Hershey bars
1 tablespoon milk
½ pint whipping cream, whipped, or ½ large carton Cool Whip
1 9-inch baked pie shell
chocolate sprinkles (optional)

Melt chocolate bars with milk in a double boiler or microwave. Cool and fold in whipped cream. Pour into pie shell and chill. Top with additional whipped cream and chocolate sprinkles.

Susie Garrett
Grand Prairie

Fresh Coconut Pie

1 fresh whole coconut (or 3 to 4 cups shredded coconut)
4 large eggs
2 cups sugar
½ cup butter, divided
2 tablespoons flour
½ teaspoon salt
2 cups evaporated milk diluted with 2 cups water (or 4 cups milk)
4 unbaked pie shells

Shell, peel, and grate coconut and set aside. Beat together eggs, sugar, and all but 2 tablespoons of the butter; then beat in flour, salt, and milk. Stir in coconut. Divide filling evenly among pie shells and dot with reserved butter. Bake at 325 degrees for about 45 minutes.

Tanya Baker
Texas City

This recipe was handed down from my great-great-grandma who lived in Alabama. It was a special pie for family gatherings. It was a lot of work getting the coconut ready. She used fresh milk and home-churned butter and fresh yard eggs back then—one hundred years ago.

Coconut pie lovers have told me this is the best coconut pie they have ever tasted!

Chocolate-Pecan Pie

½ cup butter, softened
2 eggs, beaten
2 teaspoons vanilla
1 cup sugar
½ cup flour
1 cup chocolate chips
1 cup chopped pecans
1 9-inch unbaked pie shell

In a small bowl cream butter. Add eggs and vanilla. In a separate bowl combine sugar and flour and add to butter mixture. Stir in chocolate chips and nuts. Pour into unbaked pie shell and bake at 350 degrees 45 to 50 minutes or until golden brown. Cool about 1 hour and serve warm.

Darlene Eller
Rio Vista

Macaroon Coconut Pie

1¾ cups sugar
5 eggs
1 can cream of coconut
1 cup milk
¼ cup margarine, softened or melted
½ cup plus 2 tablespoons flour
3 cups flaked coconut
2 unbaked 9-inch pie shells

Beat together sugar and eggs. Add cream of coconut, milk, and margarine. Add flour and coconut. Pour into pie shells. Bake at 400 degrees for 10 minutes, reduce heat to 350 degrees, and continue baking for 30 minutes or until brown.

Agnew Cromeans
Hempstead

Egg Custard Pie

6 eggs
2½ cups milk
1 cup sugar
nutmeg to taste
1 unbaked 9-inch pie shell

Beat eggs until mixed; add milk and sugar. Pour into unbaked pie shell and sprinkle with nutmeg. Bake at 450 degrees for 10 minutes, then reduce heat to 350 degrees and bake for 45 minutes or until set.

Nora Kincheloe
Burnet

Nora Kincheloe is a member of the SOS Sewing Club of Bertram. Established fifty years ago by Hill Country women who got together to do mending, the club was called "SOS" for "Sew Our Socks." Today the club members make quilts.

Jeff Davis Pie

1¾ cups sugar
1 tablespoon flour
½ teaspoon pumpkin pie spice
dash of nutmeg
½ cup butter
4 eggs
1 cup milk
1 tablespoon vanilla
1 unbaked 9-inch pie shell

Mix sugar, flour, and spices. Stir in butter. Beat in eggs and add milk and vanilla. Mix well. Pour into unbaked pie shell. Bake 10 to 15 minutes at 400 degrees, then reduce heat to 350 degrees and bake 30 minutes more or until pie sets.

Elizabeth Clark
Dallas

This recipe is my great-grandmother's. It was printed in a ladies' auxiliary cookbook from the 1920s under her name.

Buttermilk Pie

1½ cups sugar
½ cup Bisquick
1 cup buttermilk
⅓ cup melted butter or margarine
1 teaspoon vanilla
3 eggs

Beat together all ingredients until smooth. Pour into a greased pie pan. Bake at 350 degrees for 30 minutes or until a knife inserted in the center comes out clean.

Kathryn Martin
Midland

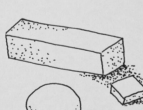

Country Chess Pie

2 cups sugar
2 heaping tablespoons flour
1 heaping tablespoon yellow cornmeal
1 stick butter or margarine, melted
3 eggs, beaten
½ cup buttermilk
2 teaspoons vanilla (or 1 teaspoon vanilla and 1 teaspoon lemon
    extract)
1 unbaked 9-inch pie shell

Combine sugar, flour, and cornmeal, mixing well. Add butter and
mix well. Add eggs and mix well. Add buttermilk and vanilla and
mix well. Pour into pie shell. Bake at 425 degrees for 10 minutes.
Reduce temperature to 325 degrees and bake for approximately
30 minutes. When pie begins to brown, place a sheet of aluminum
foil over the pie or on the rack above the pie. When done, the pie
will shake a little in the middle but not all over. Let set until cool.

Pauline Maxwell
Arlington

Company Comin' Pie

3 egg whites
1 teaspoon cream of tarter
1 cup sugar
18 soda crackers, crushed
½ cup chopped pecans
¼ cup coconut
1 teaspoon vanilla
½ pint whipping cream
2 tablespoons sugar

Combine egg whites and cream of tarter and beat until stiff. Add
sugar, crackers, pecans, vanilla, and coconut. Bake in a well-
greased pie pan at 325 degrees for 25 minutes. Cool and then top
with whipped cream to which sugar has been added. Sprinkle a
few pecans on top and chill for 6 hours.

Ruth Wood
Plainview

Fried Pies

FILLING
2 8-ounce packages dried apples, apricots, or peaches
water
2 cups sugar

PASTRY
2 cups flour
1 teaspoon salt
½ cup shortening
¾ cup milk
1 egg, beaten
oil or shortening

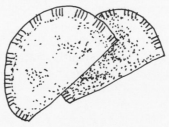

To make filling, cook fruit in water until tender. Blend in sugar. Cool. To make pastry, blend together flour, salt, and shortening. Mix egg and milk and add to flour mixture. Do not have dough too stiff. Roll out on a floured board to about ⅛ inch thick. Cut out circles using a dessert dish or saucer. Add a heaping tablespoon of cooked fruit to each circle. Fold pastry over, moisten edges with milk, and crimp with fork or fingertips. Fry in a large skillet in oil or shortening until brown on both sides. Drain on paper towels.

Ruth Perry Wickham
Mabank

This was my grandmother's recipe. In the 1930s all of her seven children and grandchildren came home to live for a while because of the Depression. We'd all congregate in the kitchen and eat fried pies as fast as she could make them.

Basic Pie Filling

1 cup sugar
⅓ cup flour
2 cups milk
2 egg yolks (save whites for meringue)
pinch of salt
1 teaspoon vanilla
1 tablespoon butter

Mix sugar and flour; add enough milk to make a thick paste. Add egg yolks and beat. Add remaining milk and salt. Mix well. Cook in a double boiler until thick. Remove from heat and add butter and vanilla. For coconut pie, add 1 cup coconut. For chocolate pie, add 2 tablespoons cocoa to sugar. For pineapple pie, add 1 cup cooked pineapple. For raisin pie, cook 1 cup raisins, drain, and add to filling.

Jewell Graham
Crockett

Fresh Peach Meringue Pie

2 pounds fresh peaches (about 2½ cups)
1 teaspoon lemon juice
½ cup sugar
3 tablespoons cornstarch
½ teaspoon cinnamon
¼ teaspoon nutmeg
¼ teaspoon salt
2 egg yolks, slightly beaten
1 9-inch graham cracker crust

MERINGUE
2 egg whites
¼ teaspoon cream of tarter
¼ cup sugar

Peel, pit, and crush peaches, then mix in lemon juice. Combine sugar, cornstarch, cinnamon, nutmeg, and salt in a double boiler. Stir in the peaches and cook over medium heat to boiling. Reduce heat to low and cook 3 minutes, stirring constantly. Stir a small amount of hot peach mixture into the egg yolks, then add to mixture. Cook until thickened, stirring constantly. Remove from heat and cool 10 minutes. Pour into graham cracker crust and cool to room temperature. To make meringue, beat egg whites and cream of tarter until soft peaks form. Gradually add sugar until stiff peaks form. Spread on top of pie. Bake at 350 degrees for about 10 minutes.

Doris Spangler
Sherman

My mother made up this recipe for fresh pumpkin pie that is not like the typical pumpkin pie. It does not have the usual spices, but the combination of butter flavoring and the coconutlike texture of the fresh pumpkin makes it an interesting dessert.

Roerock's Fresh Pumpkin Pie

2 cups mashed fresh pumpkin
1 cup evaporated milk
1 cup sugar
3 tablespoons cornstarch
pinch of salt
3 eggs, separated
2 tablespoons margarine
1 teaspoon vanilla extract
1 teaspoon butter flavoring
1 baked 9-inch pie shell
⅛ teaspoon cream of tartar
6 tablespoons sugar

Combine pumpkin, milk, sugar, cornstarch, salt, and egg yolks in a saucepan. Cook and stir over low heat until thickened. Add margarine, vanilla, and butter flavoring. Pour into baked pie shell. Beat egg whites with cream of tartar until stiff. Gradually add sugar and beat in. Spread on pie and bake at 375 degrees until browned.

Carolyn Pryor
Pettus

Delicious Pumpkin Pie with Can't-Fail Crust

CRUST
2⅛ cups all-purpose flour
½ teaspoon salt
1 cup shortening
½ cup cold milk (or water)

FILLING
4 eggs, slightly beaten
2 16-ounce cans solid-pack pumpkin
1 cup sugar
1 teaspoon salt
2½ teaspoons cinnamon
1½ teaspoons ginger
1½ teaspoons cloves
¾ teaspoon nutmeg
1 can Eagle Brand sweetened condensed milk
1 can evaporated milk

My father showed me how to make this pie crust when I was a little girl.

To make crust, mix flour and salt, then cut in shortening until mixture has the consistency of fine crumbs. Add liquid all at once and mix well (mixture will be very sticky). Divide dough in half. Flour hands and press each half into a 9-inch deep-dish pie plate until pan is covered evenly with dough; flute edges. (The more you work with the dough, the tougher it will be.)

To make filling, combine ingredients in order listed. Divide mixture evenly between pie shells. Bake at 425 degrees 15 minutes, then reduce heat to 350 degrees and bake an additional 45 minutes or until toothpick comes out clean when inserted in center of pie. Cool; garnish with whipped cream, if desired.

Tina Keel
Justin

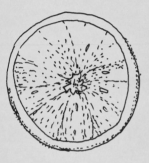

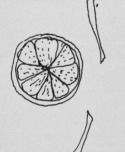

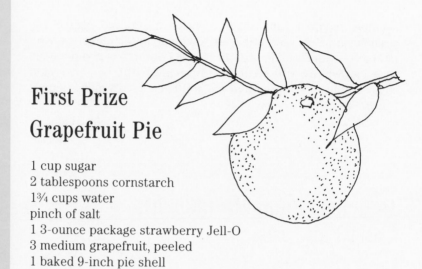

First Prize
Grapefruit Pie

1 cup sugar
2 tablespoons cornstarch
1¾ cups water
pinch of salt
1 3-ounce package strawberry Jell-O
3 medium grapefruit, peeled
1 baked 9-inch pie shell
whipped cream

Cook sugar, cornstarch, water, and salt until thick and clear. Add
Jell-O and stir until mixture begins to set. Remove membrane
from grapefruit sections, drain in a strainer, and cut into small
pieces. Add to Jell-O mixture. Pour into pie shell and top with
whipped cream. Strawberries can be substituted for grapefruit.

Cathey L. Fleming
Orange

Lemon Pie

1 large package lemon Jell-O or 2 small packages lemon Jell-O
½ cup boiling water
1 can evaporated milk, chilled
¾ cup sugar
juice of 1 lemon
zest of 1 lemon
whipped cream
2 baked pie shells or graham cracker crusts

Dissolve Jell-O in boiling water. Set aside. Whip evaporated milk
and add sugar, a little at a time. Fold Jell-O into the milk and add
lemon juice and zest. Pour into pie shells and top with whipped
cream.

W. Mapel Maddox
Dallas

Blue Ribbon Sour Cream Pear Pie

2 cups pears, peeled and diced
½ cup sugar
1 egg, beaten
1 tablespoon flour
1 cup sour cream
1 teaspoon vanilla
dash of salt
1 unbaked pie shell

CRUMB TOPPING
½ cup sugar
⅓ cup flour
¼ cup butter, softened

Combine pears, sugar, egg, flour, sour cream, vanilla, and salt. Blend gently with spatula. Spoon into unbaked pie shell. Bake at 350 degrees for 25 minutes. Combine ingredients for crumb topping, sprinkle on top of pie, and return to oven. Bake for an additional 35 minutes. Refrigerate 2 to 3 hours. Serve chilled. Great with lemonade or iced tea.

James Booth
Canyon

Yummy Meatless Mince Pie

2 cups chopped apples
1 cup chopped green tomatoes
1 teaspoon cinnamon
½ teaspoon salt
½ teaspoon allspice
½ teaspoon cloves
1½ cups sugar
½ pound raisins
⅛ cup vinegar
pastry for two 2-crust pies
milk and sugar

Mix together apples, tomatoes, salt, spices, sugar, raisins, and vinegar. Bring to a boil and simmer until thick. Pour into pie shells. Cover with top crust. Sprinkle with a little milk and sugar and bake at 350 degrees about 30 minutes or until crust is golden.

D. McKinney
Kingsbury

About twenty-five years ago I changed around an old Kerr recipe because we didn't like suet. People who hate mincemeat love this pie.

Pecan Crunch Pie

3 egg whites
1 cup sugar
1 teaspoon baking powder
1 cup graham cracker crumbs
1 teaspoon vanilla
1 cup chopped pecans
1 carton Cool Whip
peach slices (optional)

Beat egg whites until fairly stiff, then add sugar and baking powder, mix well, and add graham cracker crumbs, vanilla, and pecans. Blend well and pour into a well-greased 8- or 9-inch pie pan. Bake at 350 degrees for approximately 30 minutes. Cool and top with Cool Whip. Garnish with peach slices. Refrigerate until ready to serve.

Mary Towry
Wichita Falls

Pecan Pie

This recipe has been handed down over the years from pre–Civil War days.

½ cup butter or margarine, melted
1 cup sugar
½ cup dark corn syrup
¼ teaspoon salt
1 teaspoon vanilla
3 eggs, beaten
1½ cups chopped pecans
1 unbaked 9-inch pie shell

Add butter, sugar, corn syrup, salt, and vanilla to beaten eggs. Mix well. Fold in pecans. Mix well and pour into pie shell. Bake at 375 degrees for 45 minutes or until a toothpick inserted in the center comes out clean.

Lois Hill
Waco
Tom Tiernan
Dallas

Big Mama's Man-Killer Pie

1½ cups sugar, divided
1 stick butter
2 tablespoons flour
⅛ teaspoon salt
2 cups milk
3 eggs yolks, beaten
1 teaspoon vanilla
1 baked pie shell

MERINGUE
3 egg whites
6 tablespoons sugar
¼ teaspoon cream of tartar
½ teaspoon vanilla

Mix ¾ cup sugar and butter. Brown in a cast iron skillet until light brown. Add remaining sugar, flour, and salt. In a double boiler heat milk, then add sugar mixture and cook until heated through. Add a little bit of the warm mixture to the beaten egg yolks. Mix well, then add to the milk mixture. Cook and stir until thick. Add vanilla. Pour into baked pie shell. To make meringue, beat egg whites with vanilla and cream of tartar until soft peaks form. Gradually add sugar until stiff and glossy. Spread meringue over hot filling and seal to edges. Cook at 350 degrees about 12 to 15 minutes or until meringue is golden.

Jim Pool
Dallas

When I was growing up, I remember eating at my grandparents' house near Lindale on Sundays and holidays. My grandmother, Mag McDade, made a caramel pie which my grandfather, Ed McDade, especially loved. It was very rich, so he called it "the man-killer pie."

Preacher Man's Sweet Tater Pie

4 medium to large sweet potatoes
1 stick margarine
2 cups sugar
2 eggs
1 small can condensed milk
1 cup ribbon cane or other syrup
2 teaspoons nutmeg
2 9-inch unbaked pie shells

Boil potatoes until tender. Peel and mash. Add remaining ingredients and beat with an electric mixer until very smooth. Pour into pie shells. Bake at 350 degrees for 60 minutes.

Martin J. Alewine
Fairfield

This recipe came from W. A. Young of Centerville, who works part time at a meat-processing plant, raises hogs on his farm, and is pastor of a church in Huntsville on Sundays.

TEXAS COUNTRY
REPORTER
COOKBOOK

Kurt House has spent his life collecting and rebuilding old fans and has one of the largest private collections of fans in the country.

P eanut Butter Pie is a specialty of the Puddin Hill Store in Greenville. It is one of the best desserts I know.

Fan Man's Sweet Potato Pecan Pie

⅔ cup brown sugar
1 tablespoon unflavored gelatin
½ teaspoon salt
½ teaspoon ginger
½ teaspoon cinnamon
½ teaspoon nutmeg
1¼ cups cooked, mashed sweet potatoes
3 eggs, separated
½ cup milk
¼ teaspoon cream of tartar
½ cup granulated sugar
1 9-inch baked pie shell
sweetened whipped cream

CARAMELIZED PECANS
2 tablespoons sugar
½ cup pecan halves

In a saucepan mix brown sugar, gelatin, salt, and spices. In a separate bowl blend sweet potatoes, egg yolks, and milk; stir into sugar mixture. Cook over medium heat, stirring constantly until mixture just starts to boil. Refrigerate, stirring occasionally, until mixture mounds slightly when dropped from a spoon. Beat egg whites and cream of tartar until foamy. Beat in granulated sugar, 1 tablespoon at a time; continue beating until stiff and glossy. Do not underbeat; this step determines the texture of the pie. Fold sweet potato mixture into meringue; transfer to pie shell. Refrigerate at least 3 hours. Garnish with whipped cream and sprinkle with caramelized pecans.

To caramelize pecans, cook sugar in skillet over low heat, stirring constantly, until sugar melts and turns light brown. Stir in pecan halves, coating well. Pour into buttered shallow pan. Cool, then break into pieces.

Kurt House
Dallas

Peanut Butter Pie

1 8-ounce package cream cheese, softened
1 cup chunky peanut butter
⅔ cup powdered sugar
⅓ cup half-and-half
1 8-ounce carton whipped topping
1 graham cracker crust
½ cup heavy cream
1 tablespoon powdered sugar

Beat cream cheese, peanut butter, and powdered sugar together until smooth. Gradually add half-and-half, beating until well blended. Stir in whipped topping. Spoon into graham cracker crust. Whip cream, gradually adding powdered sugar until soft peaks form. Spoon or pipe around edge of pie. Freeze. Slice while frozen. Let stand 20 minutes before serving.

Mary Lauderdale
Greenville

Mary Lauderdale and her husband Sam have been making and selling fruitcakes in Greenville since 1955.

Pioneer Raisin Pie

1¼ cups sugar
1 stick margarine, melted
3 eggs, well beaten
2 tablespoons apple cider vinegar
¼ teaspoon allspice
¼ teaspoon cinnamon
2 cups raisins
1 unbaked pie shell

Combine sugar, margarine, eggs, vinegar, and spices and mix well. Stir in raisins. Pour into pie shell. Bake at 375 degrees for 40 minutes or until firm and brown.

Pearl Berry
Mesquite

Fresh Strawberry Pie

1 3-ounce package cream cheese, softened
1 baked 9-inch pie shell, cooled
1 quart fresh strawberries, cleaned and hulled
1 cup sugar
3 tablespoons cornstarch
Cool Whip

Spread cream cheese over bottom of cooled pie shell. Spread half of the strawberries over the cream cheese. Place remaining half of the strawberries in blender or food processor and puree until completely liquid. Add enough water to make 1½ cups liquid. Mix sugar and cornstarch and add to strawberry liquid. Cook until thickened. Pour over berries in pastry shell. Chill for 2 hours. Top with Cool Whip.

Nina Young
Emory

COBBLERS

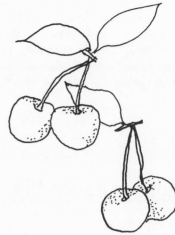

Cherry Cobbler

1 stick butter
1 cup flour
1 cup sugar
2 teaspoons baking powder
1 egg
½ cup milk
1 21-ounce can cherry pie filling
vanilla ice cream or whipped cream

Melt butter in a 9″ × 5″ × 3″ baking dish. In a separate bowl mix together dry ingredients. Add egg and milk and blend well. Pour half of the melted butter into the batter, mix well, then pour batter into the baking dish. Pour cherry pie filling into the middle of the batter. Bake at 350 degrees 35 to 40 minutes or until nicely browned. Top with vanilla ice cream or whipped cream.

Joan Bingham
Arlington

This is a very special treat for my family because they get it only once each year—when I am making grape jelly. It came about because I hated to throw away all that nice grape pulp after straining the juice off the grapes.

Texas Grape Cobbler

2 cups grape pulp (about 4 pounds grapes)
½ cup margarine
1 cup sugar
1 cup flour
1 teaspoon baking powder
1 cup milk

Prepare grapes as for making juice or jelly. Strain off the juice, then mash the remaining pulp through a colander and discard seeds. Melt margarine in a 9-inch square cake pan. Mix sugar, flour, baking powder, and milk. Pour over the melted butter. Pour grape pulp over the batter. With the blade of a table knife, cut pulp into the batter several times in each direction. Bake at 350 degrees for 45 to 50 minutes or until crust is browned. Serve warm with vanilla ice cream.

Carol Ellis
Friona

Stonewall Peach Cobbler

FILLING
2 to 2½ cups sugar
½ cup cornstarch
8 cups sliced fresh peaches
½ teaspoon almond extract
¼ cup melted butter

PASTRY
2 cups flour
2 tablespoons sugar
pinch of salt
½ cup shortening
4 tablespoons ice water
½ cup melted butter
¼ cup sugar

To make filling, combine sugar and cornstarch and toss with peaches. Add almond extract and butter and set aside. To make pastry, combine flour, sugar, and salt. Cut shortening into flour until mixture is the consistency of cornmeal. Gradually add ice water until dough holds its shape. Roll out on a floured board and cut into strips. Pour peach filling into a buttered 9″ × 13″ pan. Crisscross dough strips over filling. Brush pastry with melted butter and sprinkle with sugar. Bake at 400 degrees for 30 minutes or until crust is brown.

Matthew Kast
Fredericksburg

Washday Cobbler

1 stick margarine
2 cups sugar, divided
¾ cup milk
1 cup flour
2 teaspoons baking powder
dash of salt
2 to 4 cups fruit (berries, peaches, apples, etc.)

Melt butter in a baking dish. In a separate bowl mix 1 cup sugar, milk, flour, baking powder, and salt and pour over butter. Top with fruit. Sprinkle with remaining 1 cup sugar. Bake at 325 to 350 degrees for 30 to 45 minutes.

Norma Read
Franklin

My mother, Annie Violet Graves, cooked this dish in the 1940s for peanut thresher crews. We lived on the North Fork of the Double Mountain Fork of the Brazos River where we picked wild plums. Plums that were not used for fresh cobblers were canned in quart and gallon jars to be made into jam, jelly, or cobblers at a later date.

Brazos River Plum Cobbler

½ stick butter or margarine
1 cup sugar
1 cup all-purpose flour
2 teaspoons baking powder
dash of salt
¾ cup milk
2 to 3 cups ripe wild plums (or any small tart plums)
1 cup sugar
1 teaspoon lemon juice
½ cup water

Melt butter in 8″ × 10″ × 2″ baking dish. In a separate bowl combine sugar, flour, baking powder, salt, and milk. Pour into buttered baking dish. Wash and remove stems from plums. In a saucepan heat plums, sugar, lemon juice, and water until mixture comes to a boil. Then gently pour over batter but do not stir. Bake at 350 degrees for 45 minutes or until top is browned. Serve hot with thick cow's cream or whipped cream. Remember to watch for seeds.

Willa Faye Didway
Post

Cranberry Cobbler

1⅓ cups sugar, divided
1¼ cups water
1 teaspoon vanilla
4 tablespoons butter or margarine, divided
¾ cup all-purpose flour
1¼ teaspoons baking powder
½ teaspoon salt
⅓ cup sugar
½ cup milk
1 cup fresh or frozen cranberries, cut in half

In a small saucepan combine 1 cup sugar, water, vanilla, and 2 tablespoons butter. Bring to a boil, stirring constantly. Remove from heat and pour into an 8-inch square dish. In a separate bowl combine flour, baking powder, salt, and remaining ⅓ cup sugar. Cut in remaining 2 tablespoons butter. Stir in milk; fold in cranberries. Spoon cranberry mixture evenly over sugar mixture. Bake at 375 degrees for 30 to 35 minutes.

Stanley B. Gregory
Joshua

PUDDINGS

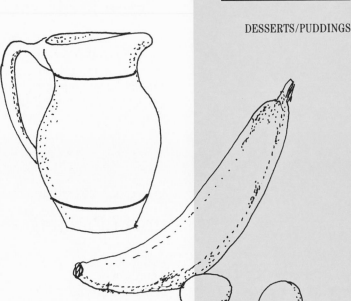

Banana Pudding

½ cup sugar
⅓ cup flour
¼ teaspoon salt
2 cups milk, scalded
2 egg yolks
1 teaspoon vanilla
3 bananas, sliced
18 vanilla wafers
2 egg whites
⅓ cup sugar
½ teaspoon cornstarch

Blend sugar, flour, salt, and milk. Cook over hot water or in double boiler until thick, stirring constantly. Cover and cook for 15 minutes. Beat egg yolks slightly, then add custard gradually. Return to double boiler and cook 2 minutes. Cover and cool, then add vanilla. Line baking dish with vanilla wafers and sliced bananas alternately. Cover with custard. Beat egg whites until stiff, adding cornstarch and sugar gradually until thick, then spread over custard. Make peaks in meringue with bottom of spoon. Bake at 325 degrees for 20 minutes. Serves 6.

Gordon Lee
Smithville

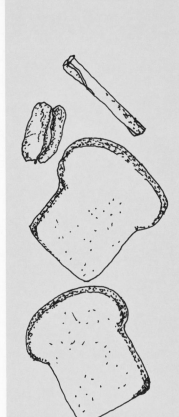

Bread Pudding Extra

4 to 6 slices wheat bread, cubed or torn
½ teaspoon cinnamon
1 cup muesli-style cereal
1½ cups milk
1 stick butter or margarine
4 eggs
½ cup white sugar
½ cup brown sugar
1 teaspoon vanilla
½ cup chopped pecans (optional)
½ cup shredded coconut (optional)

Place bread pieces in a well-greased 8″ × 8″ × 2″ baking dish. Sprinkle with cinnamon and cover with an even layer of cereal. Set aside. Heat milk and butter until butter melts. Beat eggs, sugars, and vanilla together and slowly add to sugar mixture. Pour gently over bread and cereal. Top with nuts and coconut. Let stand at least 5 minutes. Place dish in a pan of water that comes halfway up the sides of the dish. Bake at 350 degrees for 30 to 35 minutes.

Linda E. Montrose
Frankston

This recipe goes back to the early 1800s. I was raised on it and was able to get my 90-year-old aunt to give me the recipe. It was prepared often, especially during the Great Depression.

Bread Pudding

3 eggs
1 cup sugar
2½ cups milk, heated
about 8 biscuits
1 teaspoon vanilla
dash of nutmeg

POOR-DO SAUCE
1 tablespoon flour dissolved in a little water
1½ cups water
½ cup sugar
1 tablespoon butter
dash of nutmeg

Beat eggs well, then add sugar and milk. Pour over crumbled biscuits. Add vanilla and nutmeg. Bake at 350 degrees until done. Top with Poor-Do Sauce. To make sauce, mix all ingredients in a saucepan and cook until thickened.

Jo Hunt
Dodson

Persimmon Pudding

2 cups persimmon pulp
2 cups sugar
3 eggs, beaten
1¼ cups buttermilk
2 cups flour
1 teaspoon baking powder
1 teaspoon baking soda
½ teaspoon cinnamon
3 tablespoons butter, melted

Mix all ingredients except butter, then add butter to mixture. Pour into a 9″ × 13″ pan. Bake at 350 degrees for 30 to 35 minutes. Serve warm with Cool Whip.

Juanita Seagraves
Somerville

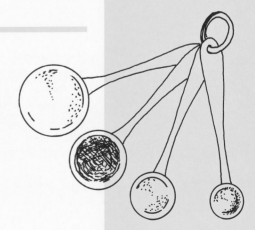

Piggy Pudding

¼ cup butter
1 cup sugar
2 eggs
2 squares chocolate
1 cup milk
1 teaspoon vanilla
1 cup flour
2 teaspoons baking powder

Cream together butter and sugar. Add eggs and beat. Melt chocolate in milk and add to butter and sugar mixture. Add vanilla, flour, and baking powder. Pour into a deep 9″ × 9″ pan. Bake at 350 degrees for 20 minutes. Check for doneness with toothpick inserted near edge (middle will be gooey). Serve warm with vanilla ice cream. Serves 6.

Sharon Van Tyne
Plano

Date Pudding

1 cup brown sugar
1½ cups white sugar, divided
1½ cups hot water
1 teaspoon vanilla
dash of salt
1 cup flour
½ cup chopped dates
1 cup chopped nuts
1 heaping teaspoon baking powder
1 cup milk

Combine brown sugar, ½ cup white sugar, hot water, vanilla, and salt in an 8″ × 8″ baking dish. Stir until sugars are dissolved. In a separate bowl combine remaining 1 cup sugar, flour, dates, nuts, baking powder, and milk. Mix well and pour over sugar mixture, but do not stir. Bake at 350 degrees for about 45 minutes or until done.

Angie Gaisford
Shattuck, Oklahoma

English Plum Pudding

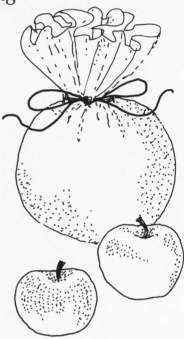

3 cups flour
1 teaspoon baking soda
½ teaspoon salt
buttermilk
3 eggs
1 cup chopped suet
1 cup raisins
1 cup currants
2 cups chopped apples
½ cup molasses (optional)

HOT SAUCE
2 cups milk
¼ stick butter or margarine
½ teaspoon nutmeg
½ cup brown sugar
½ teaspoon cinnamon

COLD SAUCE
1 quart milk
2 eggs
2 cups sugar
1 teaspoon vanilla
1 teaspoon nutmeg

This was originally Grandma Mary Blandford's recipe. She came to Texas from England in 1880, landing at the site of old Indianola.

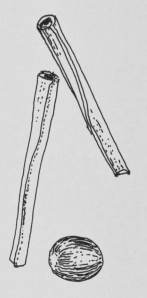

Mix together flour, soda, and salt. Add enough buttermilk to make a soft dough and mix well. Mix in eggs and remaining ingredients. Wet a clean cloth and wring dry. Sprinkle flour on one side, place ball of dough on cloth, draw cloth up tight, and tie tightly with string. Place a saucer in the bottom of a large pot, fill with water, and bring to a boil. Rest pudding on plate and boil 2 hours, adding more boiling water if needed. Serve sliced and topped with hot or cold sauce. To make sauces, mix ingredients together and bring to a boil.

Hazel Blandford
San Antonio

Cabinet Pudding

1 envelope unflavored gelatin
½ cup cold water
½ cup boiling water
6 eggs, separated
1 cup sugar
1 cup wine
1 cup maraschino cherries, halved
1 cup chopped pecans
2 dozen macaroons, broken into pieces

Dissolve gelatin in cold water, then add boiling water. Mix well. Beat egg yolks well, add sugar and wine, and cook until thick. Add gelatin and bring to a boil. In a bowl combine cherries, pecans, and macaroons. Add gelatin mixture and beat well. Beat egg whites and fold into mixture. Refrigerate until firm. Serve with whipped cream.

Ann Niethamer
El Paso

Cabinet Pudding is a traditional dish we serve at Christmas dinner. The recipe came from my grandmother, who lived in Stockdale.

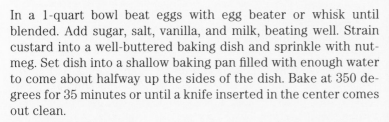

Beryl's Egg Custard

4 eggs
½ cup sugar
½ teaspoon salt
1 teaspoon vanilla
2 cups milk
½ teaspoon nutmeg

In a 1-quart bowl beat eggs with egg beater or whisk until blended. Add sugar, salt, vanilla, and milk, beating well. Strain custard into a well-buttered baking dish and sprinkle with nutmeg. Set dish into a shallow baking pan filled with enough water to come about halfway up the sides of the dish. Bake at 350 degrees for 35 minutes or until a knife inserted in the center comes out clean.

Paula Bradley
Alvarado

Guadalajara Flan

1 cup sugar
1 can sweetened condensed milk
14 ounces milk
4 eggs
1 3-ounce package cream cheese, softened
⅛ teaspoon Mexican vanilla or 1 teaspoon regular vanilla

Melt sugar in a heavy iron skillet. Do not burn! Pour caramelized sugar into a Pyrex casserole dish. Combine remaining ingredients in a blender and process until smooth. Pour over sugar. Cover pan with aluminum foil and secure with a rubber band. Place dish in pan of water and bake at 325 degrees for at least 1 hour or until a knife inserted in the middle comes out clean. Chill and invert on platter before serving. Serve with whipped cream or fresh strawberries.

Christine Zunker
Fort Worth

This classic Mexican dessert looks beautiful and has become a Christmas tradition in my family. It takes only 10 minutes to prepare.

ICE CREAM

Homemade Ice Cream

3 scant cups sugar
3 tablespoons cornstarch
¾ teaspoon salt
2 quarts milk, divided
5 eggs, well beaten
1 pint cream
2 tablespoons vanilla
1 tablespoon lemon extract

Mix sugar, cornstarch, salt, and about ⅔ quart milk. Bring to a boil and cook 3 minutes, stirring constantly. Pour boiling mixture slowly into beaten eggs and beat well. Add remaining milk, cream, vanilla, and lemon extract. Strain into freezer container and freeze according to manufacturer's instructions.

Judie Morris
Euless

Peach Ice Cream

3 cups peach pulp
juice of 3 lemons
juice of 1 large orange
3 cups sugar
1 teaspoon vanilla
milk
cream or half-and-half

Mix peach pulp, juices, sugar, and vanilla. Set aside at room temperature for 3 hours. Add milk and cream and mix well. Pour into freezer container and freeze according to manufacturer's instructions.

Linda Wheatley
Garland

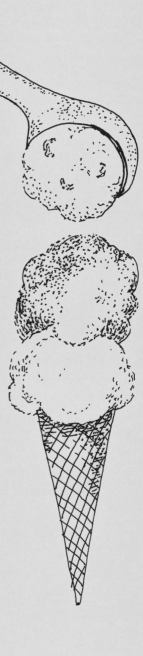

Chocolate Ice Cream

1 can Eagle Brand milk
5 eggs, beaten
2 cups sugar
1 tablespoon vanilla
chocolate milk

Mix milk, eggs, sugar, vanilla, and enough chocolate milk to fill freezer container. Freeze according to manufacturer's instructions.

Olivia Harrington
Duncanville

Milky Way Ice Cream

12 Milky Way candy bars
1 can Eagle Brand milk
1 quart half-and-half
1 ounce chocolate syrup
milk

Combine candy bars and Eagle Brand milk in a double boiler and heat until bars are melted. Cool. Add half-and-half, chocolate syrup, and enough milk to fill the freezer container. Freeze according to manufacturer's instructions.

Janie L. Pike
Leona

Pineapple Sherbet

3 egg whites
2 cups sugar
1 quart buttermilk
1 quart whole milk
juice of 3 lemons or 1 package lemonade Kool-Aid
1 No. 2 can crushed pineapple

Beat egg whites and add sugar. Add remaining ingredients and mix well. Pour into freezer container and freeze according to manufacturer's instructions.

Joan McCorkle
San Antonio

Cranberry Ice

4 cups fresh cranberries
3 cups water
2 cups sugar
⅛ teaspoon salt
½ cup orange juice

Cook cranberries and water together for 10 minutes. Add sugar, salt, and orange juice, stirring until sugar is dissolved. Put mixture through a coarse sieve or food mill, forcing through as much pulp as possible. Turn into a refrigerator tray and freeze. When mushy, transfer to a chilled bowl and beat with a rotary beater until light and fluffy. Return to refrigerator tray and freeze until firm. Serve as a meat accompaniment or with cookies as a dessert.

Mrs. R. W. Burns
Keller

Hot Fudge Topping for Ice Cream

1 cup sugar
4 tablespoons cocoa
3 tablespoons cornstarch
pinch of salt
1 cup boiling water
2 tablespoons margarine

Combine sugar, cocoa, cornstarch, salt, and boiling water. Boil until thick, stirring constantly. Add margarine, stirring until melted.

Marilyn Fink
Arlington

ASSORTED DESSERTS

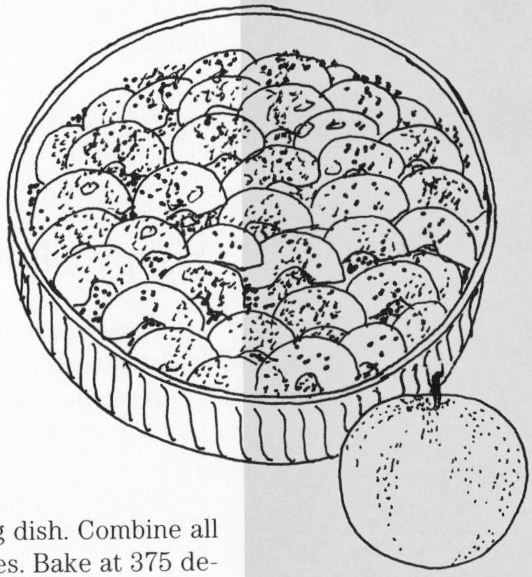

Texas Apple Crumb

2 20-ounce cans apple pie filling
¾ cup brown sugar
½ cup all-purpose flour
½ cup oats
⅓ cup butter or margarine, softened
¾ teaspoon cinnamon
½ teaspoon nutmeg

Place apple filling in a greased 1-quart baking dish. Combine all remaining ingredients and sprinkle over apples. Bake at 375 degrees for 30 minutes. Serve warm. Serves 6.

Betty Thayer
Crowley

Brandied Fruit

FIRST WEEK
1 package dry yeast
1 cup diced and drained peaches
1 cup sugar, divided
¼ cup drained maraschino cherries

SECOND WEEK
1 cup diced and drained pineapple
1 cup sugar
¼ cup drained maraschino cherries

THIRD WEEK
1 cup drained pears or apricots
1 cup sugar
¼ cup drained maraschino cherries

In a large glass jar mix together yeast, peaches, sugar, and maraschino cherries. Stir well and cover loosely. Let stand at room temperature for one week. Add pineapple, sugar, and maraschino cherries to mixture in jar. Let stand for one week. Add pears, sugar, and maraschino cherries to mixture in jar and let stand one week. As mixture is used, add more fruit on a rotating basis, beginning with the first week's ingredients. Store at room temperature.

Norma Haddock
McGregor

Puppy Chow

1 12-ounce package chocolate chips
1 stick margarine
1 cup peanut butter
1 large box Crispex cereal
1 1-pound box powdered sugar

Melt chocolate chips, margarine, and peanut butter. Mix well and pour over cereal, stirring very gently. Pour powdered sugar in a large paper bag, add cereal mixture, and shake gently to coat well. Store in a covered container.

Donna Holbrooks
Springtown

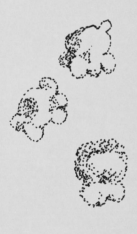

Caramel Corn

2¼ cups brown sugar, divided
¼ cup boiling water
2 sticks butter or margarine
½ cup white corn syrup
1 teaspoon salt
1 teaspoon butter flavoring
½ teaspoon baking soda
8 quarts popped corn

Sprinkle ¼ cup brown sugar in the bottom of a heavy skillet; cook until burned. Add boiling water and set aside. In a saucepan combine 1 tablespoon of the reserved burnt sugar with the remaining

2 cups brown sugar, margarine, corn syrup, salt, and butter flavoring and bring to a boil. Boil 5 minutes. Remove from heat and stir in soda. Pour over popped corn, mixing with a fork. Divide among three large cake pans and bake at 250 degrees for 1 hour. Stir two or three times during cooking to distribute syrup evenly. Cool and break in bite-size pieces. Store in airtight containers.

Mrs. George Cathcart
Humble

Candied Corn and Nuts

5 quarts freshly popped popcorn, unsalted
2 cups roasted peanuts
2 cups pecan halves
1 cup margarine
2 cups packed brown sugar
½ cup dark corn syrup
½ teaspoon baking soda
½ teaspoon salt
½ teaspoon vanilla

Combine popcorn and nuts in a lightly greased roasting pan. Melt margarine in a large saucepan, then stir in sugar and syrup. Bring to a boil and boil 5 minutes, stirring occasionally. Remove from heat and stir in soda, salt, and vanilla. Pour over popcorn, stirring to coat evenly. Bake at 250 degrees for 1 hour, stirring every 15 minutes. Cool; store in airtight containers.

Doris Crockett
Farmers Branch

Pumpkin Cheesecake

1 8-ounce package cream cheese
½ cup sugar
2 eggs
1 teaspoon vanilla
1 unbaked 9-inch deep-dish pie shell
1 16-ounce can pumpkin
1 14-ounce can sweetened condensed milk
½ teaspoon cinnamon
½ teaspoon nutmeg
½ teaspoon ginger
1 carton Cool Whip

In a large bowl, combine cream cheese, sugar, 1 egg, and vanilla. Blend until smooth. Spread over bottom of pie shell. In a medium bowl, mix together remaining ingredients except Cool Whip; spoon over cream cheese filling. Bake at 375 degrees for 50 to 55 minutes. Cool, then refrigerate several hours or overnight. Top with Cool Whip.

Mae Johonnesson
Livingston

Lemon–Cream Cheese Torte

30 single graham crackers
½ cup melted butter
1 package lemon Jell-O
1 cup hot water
1 8-ounce package cream cheese
1 teaspoon vanilla
¾ cup sugar
1 can evaporated milk

Crush graham crackers and mix with melted butter. Press into a 9″ × 13″ pan, reserving some for topping. In a small bowl dissolve Jell-O in hot water; chill and whip. In a separate bowl, mix cream cheese, vanilla, and sugar and set aside. In a large mixing bowl, whip evaporated milk. Add cream cheese mixture and whipped Jell-O. Pour into pan and garnish with reserved graham cracker mixture. Refrigerate.

Marian T. Kudlicki
Richardson

Chocolate Cheesecake

¾ cup graham cracker crumbs
1 tablespoon butter or margarine, melted
1 tablespoon sugar
2 8-ounce packages cream cheese
¾ cup sugar
⅓ cup cocoa
1 teaspoon vanilla
2 eggs
1 cup sour cream
2 tablespoons sugar
1 teaspoon vanilla
melted chocolate
fresh strawberries

Mix graham cracker crumbs, butter, and sugar and pat evenly into a 9-inch springform pan. Combine cream cheese, ¾ cup sugar, cocoa, vanilla, and eggs. Mix until creamy. Pour into crust. Bake at 375 degrees 30 minutes. Remove from oven and cool for 15 minutes. Increase oven temperature to 425 degrees. Mix sour cream, 2 tablespoons sugar, and vanilla. Spread over cooled cheesecake and return to oven. Bake 10 minutes. Cool, remove rim, and chill. Drizzle with melted chocolate and decorate with fresh strawberries before serving.

Barbara J. Helmick
Richardson

Cheesecake

1 package butter cake mix
3 eggs
1 stick margarine at room temperature
1 cup chopped pecans
1 8-ounce package cream cheese
1 package powdered sugar
fresh strawberries

Blend together cake mix, 2 eggs, margarine, and pecans and pat into the bottom of a buttered 9″ × 13″ pan. Mix cream cheese, powdered sugar, and remaining egg and spread over cake mixture. Bake at 350 degrees for 30 to 45 minutes. Cut into squares and garnish each square with a fresh strawberry.

Gilbert Beddingfield
Greenville

This recipe won first place at both the World's Fair in San Antonio as well as the Hunt County Fair.

Gilbert Beddingfield is a model builder who has constructed a miniature cotton gin that actually operates.

Easy Ice Cream Cake

2¼ cups crumbled macaroons, divided
3 cups chocolate ice cream, slightly softened
5 Heath candy bars, crushed
4 tablespoons chocolate syrup
3 tablespoons coffee liqueur (optional)
3 cups vanilla ice cream, slightly softened
whipped cream (optional)
maraschino cherries (optional)

Layer the bottom of an 8-inch springform pan with 1¼ cups macaroon crumbs. Spread chocolate ice cream evenly over crumbs. Sprinkle 4 Heath bars over the ice cream. Dribble with 3 tablespoons chocolate syrup and 2 tablespoons coffee liqueur.

Cover with remaining 1 cup macaroon crumbs and layer vanilla ice cream over macaroons. Top with remaining Heath bar, chocolate syrup, and coffee liqueur. Cover and freeze at least 8 hours or overnight. Garnish with whipped cream stars squeezed through a pastry bag and maraschino cherries. To serve, run the blade of a kitchen knife around the edges of the pan, remove the sides, and place cake on a serving platter. Slice and serve with crisp butter cookies and piping hot coffee.

Marsha Lee
Gatesville

Edible Dirt

2 large boxes instant French vanilla pudding mix
1 8-ounce package cream cheese
½ stick margarine, softened
1 cup powdered sugar
1 large package Oreo cookies, crushed

Mix pudding according to package directions, using 1 cup less milk. Let set for a few minutes. Mix together cream cheese, margarine, and powdered sugar and add to pudding mix. Line a medium-size flower pot with foil or saran wrap. Place a layer of pudding mix in flower pot, then cookies; alternate layers, ending with cookies. Place an artificial flower in the center of the pot and gummy worms (candy) on top of cookies. Serve by the spoonful. This is delicious and a lot of fun.

Mrs. M. L. McCoy
Bullard

When I was first introduced to this recipe, I was very hesitant to try it because it seemed like a good way to ruin a batch of biscuits. But I did and have been hooked on it ever since.

Chocolate Gravy

1 cup sugar
2 tablespoons cocoa
2 tablespoons flour
1 cup milk
2 tablespoons butter
2 teaspoons vanilla

Mix together dry ingredients, then add milk, butter, and vanilla. Cook in a double boiler until thick. Serve over biscuits.

Jayne Smith
McKinney

Cookies & Cream Cake

1 package Oreo cookies
¼ cup butter
½ gallon vanilla ice cream, softened
1 6-ounce package chocolate chips
1 5-ounce can evaporated milk
3 tablespoons butter
1 tablespoon vanilla
½ cup pecans
1 large carton Cool Whip
pecans

Crush 28 Oreo cookies and add to butter. Mix well and pat into a 9″ × 13″ cake pan. Freeze. Beat ice cream with an electric mixer and spread over cookie layer. Freeze. Melt chocolate chips, then add evaporated milk, butter, vanilla, and pecans. Let cool and spread over ice cream. Freeze. Spread Cool Whip over chocolate mixture, sprinkle with pecans, and freeze overnight.

LuDean Walston
Dallas

Molded Jell-O Dessert

1 large box strawberry Jell-O
2 cups hot water
1 16-ounce can crushed pineapple
2 cups whole frozen strawberries, thawed and halved
2 bananas, sliced
1 8-ounce package cream cheese
1 8-ounce carton sour cream
1 cup sugar

Mix Jell-O with hot water. Cool slightly. Drain pineapple and reserve juice, adding enough water to make 1 cup. Mix pineapple and pineapple juice with Jell-O, then fold in strawberries and bananas. Let set overnight. Before serving, mix together cream cheese, sour cream, and sugar and beat until smooth. Spread evenly over top of Jell-O.

Norma Baldridge
Mesquite

Edna Talty, who lives in one of the most highly developed parts of Dallas, has a nationally registered wildlife habitat in her backyard.

Mincemeat Dessert

mincemeat
1 small package cake mix
½ cup oats
½ cup chopped pecans
margarine

Spread mincemeat over the bottom of a baking dish or spoon into custard cups. Combine cake mix, oats, and pecans. Sprinkle generously over mincemeat. Cover dry ingredients completely with thin slices of margarine. Bake at 375 degrees for 30 minutes.

Edna Talty
Dallas

Pizza Pie Delight

1 roll sugar cookie dough or enough to cover a pizza pan
1 8-ounce package cream cheese
⅓ to ½ cup sugar
fresh or canned fruit

Spread cookie dough ⅛ inch thick over pizza pan. Bake at 350 degrees for 12 minutes. Cool. Mix cream cheese and sugar and spread over the cookie crust. Top with well-drained canned fruit or fresh fruit cut in wedges.

Helen Emery
Abilene

Punch Bowl Cake

1 package yellow cake mix
2 cans cherry pie filling
4 4-ounce boxes instant vanilla pudding mix
1 16-ounce can pineapple chunks
4 bananas, sliced and dipped in lemon juice
1 16-ounce carton Cool Whip
pecans
maraschino cherries
coconut

Prepare cake mix in layers according to directions on package. Cut layers into cubes. In a clear punch bowl, place half the cake cubes. Cover with 1 can pie filling, half the pudding, half the pineapples, and half the bananas. Top with half the Cool Whip. Repeat layers using remaining ingredients. Garnish with chopped pecans, cherries, and coconut. Chill until ready to serve.

Joyce Hamilton
Breckenridge

Blueberry Delight

1 cup flour
1 stick margarine, softened
½ cup brown sugar
½ cup chopped pecans
1 8-ounce package cream cheese, softened
2 cups powdered sugar
1 8-ounce carton Cool Whip
1 can blueberry pie filling
½ teaspoon almond flavoring

Mix flour with margarine and add brown sugar and pecans. Spread over the bottom of a jelly-roll pan. Bake at 350 degrees for 10 minutes, stir, and bake 3 more minutes, stirring twice. Press immediately into a 9″ × 13″ pan. Mix cream cheese and powdered sugar, blending well. Add Cool Whip 1 cup at a time. Drop by small spoonfuls over warm crumb layer. Let soften and spread over crumb layer. Add almond flavoring to blueberries while still in can and then spoon over cream cheese layer. Chill before serving.

Pat Emrick
Mt. Pleasant

Cherry Supreme

1½ cups flour
1½ sticks margarine
3 tablespoons sugar
1 cup chopped pecans
1 8-ounce package cream cheese
2 cups powdered sugar
2 packages Dream Whip, prepared according to directions on
    package
1 can cherry pie filling

Mix together flour, margarine, sugar, and pecans and pat into a 9″ × 13″ pan. Bake at 350 degrees for 25 minutes. Cool. Mix cream cheese and powdered sugar and fold into Dream Whip. Spread over cooled crust. Spread cherry pie filling over cream cheese mixture and refrigerate. Cut into squares and serve.

Evelyn Barnard
Levelland

Texas Yum-Yum

1 stick margarine
1 cup pecans
1 cup flour
1 6-ounce package cream cheese
1 cup powdered sugar
1 large carton Cool Whip
1 4-ounce box instant vanilla pudding mix
2 4-ounce boxes instant chocolate pudding mix
4½ cups milk
pecans (optional)

Cream together margarine, pecans, and flour. Press into a 9″ × 13″ pan and bake at 350 degrees for 20 minutes. Cool. Combine cream cheese, powdered sugar, and half the carton of Cool Whip. Mix well and spread over the cooled crust. Mix together pudding mixes and milk and pour over cream cheese layer. Spread with remaining Cool Whip and sprinkle with pecans.

Shirley Baumann
LaVernia

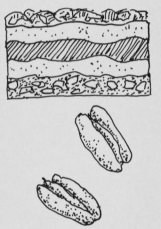

Sputniks are round balls of fried dough about the size of a fifty-cent piece. Fatkuchen, as they are called in German, were an annual Christmas treat at my grandmother's.

Sputniks

2 quarts lard
2 eggs
½ cup margarine
¾ cup sugar
1 cup milk
1 tablespoon grated orange rind
½ teaspoon salt
2 teaspoons baking powder
about 4 cups flour
1 cup currants

In a 4-quart saucepan, heat lard. (The lard is ready when a 1-inch bread cube fries but does not burn when dropped into lard.) In a large mixing bowl, beat eggs until smooth. Add margarine and sugar and mix continuously. Mix milk and orange rind and add to egg mixture. In a separate bowl, combine salt, baking powder, and flour. Sift flour mixture into egg mixture to make a stiff dough. Add currants and mix well. Drop dough in rounded teaspoons into the hot lard. Turn with a fork and fry until all sides are brown. Remove from lard and let cool. Makes about 5 dozen.

Brenda Lincke Fisseler
Hallettsville

Praline Sauce

1½ cups brown sugar
⅔ cup light corn syrup
½ cup butter or margarine
¾ cup chopped pecans
1 5-ounce can evaporated milk

In a saucepan mix sugar, syrup, and butter and bring to a boil. Cool. Add pecans and milk, blending thoroughly. Refrigerate. Yields 3 cups.

Charlotte Henry
Thomaston

COOKIES

Buffalo Chips

1 pound butter
2 cups brown sugar
2 cups white sugar
4 eggs, well beaten
4 cups flour
2 teaspoons baking powder
2 teaspoons baking soda
2 teaspoons vanilla
1 cup chopped pecans
2 cups oats
3 cups Post Toasties
1 cup coconut
1 6-ounce package semisweet chocolate chips
1 6-ounce package milk chocolate chips
1 6-ounce package butterscotch chips

Cream butter and sugars. Add eggs, flour, baking powder, baking soda, and vanilla. Mix well. Add remaining ingredients and blend well. Chill in refrigerator for 2 hours. Drop by tablespoons onto ungreased cookie sheet. Bake at 350 degrees for 10 to 12 minutes or until slightly browned.

Saundra Perry
Dallas

Cowboy Cookies

2¼ cups white sugar
2¼ cups brown sugar
2¼ cups margarine
5 eggs
2¼ teaspoons vanilla
4½ cups flour
1¼ teaspoons salt
2½ teaspoons baking soda
4½ cups oats
1 12-ounce package chocolate chips
2 cups chopped nuts

Cream together sugars, margarine, eggs, and vanilla. Add flour, salt, and baking soda. Stir in oats, chocolate chips, and nuts. Drop onto cookie sheet using an ice cream scoop. Bake at 375 degrees about 12 or 13 minutes or until done. Makes 4 to 6 dozen.

Zelna McKamie
Trophy Club

Icebox Cookies

3 cups flour
1 teaspoon baking soda
1 cup brown sugar
1 cup butter, slightly softened
1 egg
1 cup chopped pecans
1 teaspoon vanilla

Mix all ingredients together with hands. Divide into three equal portions and make into rolls, approximately 1½ inches in diameter. Wrap rolls in waxed paper and refrigerate at least 3 hours or overnight. Slice and bake at 375 degrees until lightly brown.

Karen Marotta
Mesquite

My grandparents, Albin and Louise Petter of West, were married in 1932. During that first year Granny saw a recipe in the newspaper for icebox cookies that sounded good and, more important, inexpensive to make. Four children, twenty grandchildren, and sixteen great-grandchildren later she still makes these icebox cookies.

Sugar Cookies

2 sticks margarine
¾ cup vegetable oil
2 cups sugar
2 eggs
2 teaspoons baking soda
2 teaspoons cream of tartar
5 cups flour
2 teaspoons vanilla

Cream together margarine, oil, and sugar. Add egg. Sift flour, soda, and cream of tartar. Add to sugar mixture, then add vanilla. Blend well. Chill in refrigerator at least six hours. Form dough into balls (about ½ teaspoon each) and place on ungreased cookie sheet. Flatten with glass dipped in sugar. Bake at 350 degrees for 8 to 10 minutes, or until browned. Yields 12 dozen.

Era Berrier
Madisonville

This recipe was given to my mother, Bertha Loeffler Neal, in the late 1920s. The original made three times the quantity of this one. Since this dough keeps well without refrigeration, Mother would mix the dough but cook only a small batch of cookies at a time—usually after she had baked our breakfast biscuits in the wood-burning stove. These cookies were a favorite of mine as well as of my brother and sister in our growing-up years, and continue to be favorites of our own families.

Ginger Cookies

⅔ cup shortening
⅔ cup sugar
⅔ cup dark molasses
about 4 cups flour
1 tablespoon ginger
⅓ teaspoon salt
⅓ cup water
1 tablespoon baking soda
sugar

Cream shortening; add sugar, then molasses. Sift 2 cups flour with ginger and salt. Dissolve soda in water. To shortening and sugar mixture add flour mixture alternately with liquid mixture, then add more flour (about 2 cups) until dough can be handled. Form into small balls, flatten between palms, and then dip in sugar. Place sugar side up on greased cookie sheet. Bake at 350 degrees about 10 minutes. For soft cookies, place cooled cookies in closed container with a slice of apple or bread. Yields 5 dozen.

Elza Mae Neal Fair
Weatherford

Ranger Cookies

1 cup butter
1 cup white sugar
1 cup brown sugar
1 egg
1 cup salad oil
3½ cups sifted all-purpose flour
1 teaspoon baking soda
1 teaspoon salt
1 teaspoon vanilla
1 cup oats
1 cup crushed cornflakes
½ cup shredded coconut
½ cup chopped pecans

Cream together butter and sugars until fluffy and light. Add egg, mixing well, then add salad oil, mixing well. Add flour, soda, salt, and vanilla. Add remaining ingredients. Mix well and form into walnut-sized balls. Place on an ungreased cookie sheet; flatten with a fork dipped in water. Bake at 325 degrees for 12 minutes. Cool slightly before removing from pan. For extra sweetness, sprinkle warm cookies with granulated sugar. Makes 8 dozen.

Dorothy Carpenter
Beeville

Chocolate Oatmeal Cookies

2 cups sugar
3 tablespoons cocoa
1 stick butter or margarine
1 teaspoon vanilla
½ cup milk
½ cup peanut butter
2 to 3 cups quick oats
½ cup chopped nuts (optional)

In a saucepan combine sugar, cocoa, butter, vanilla, and milk and heat over low heat until butter melts. Stir well. Bring to a boil and boil 1 minute. Add peanut butter, oats, and nuts. Pour into a buttered 9″ × 13″ pan. Cool and cut into squares before serving.

Iva Dee Fuller
Big Sandy

Iva Dee Fuller is a farmer in Big Sandy. For the past fifteen years, she has managed her forty-acre farm alone. She drives a tractor, hand-milks the cows, and plows the garden with a jenny mule.

Tec's Date Pinwheel Cookies

1½ cups chopped dates
¼ cup sugar
½ cup water
1 tablespoon lemon juice
1¾ cups flour
½ teaspoon baking powder
1 teaspoon salt
½ cup shortening
1 cup packed brown sugar
1 egg, lightly beaten
1 teaspoon vanilla

In a saucepan, cook dates, sugar, water, and lemon juice until well blended. Set aside to cool. Sift together flour, baking powder, and salt. In a separate bowl cream shortening and brown sugar. Add egg and vanilla and mix well. Add flour mixture and blend well. Roll out dough on waxed paper. Gently spread reserved date filling over the cookie dough. Use the waxed paper to assist in rolling up dough and filling, jelly-roll style. Refrigerate overnight. Slice into ¼-inch-thick slices. Place on a well-greased cookie sheet. Bake at 350 degrees for 12 to 15 minutes.

Jacqueline V. Anderson
Houston

One taste of these and date-haters will line up for more.

This recipe is from my grandmother, Madge Westfall. At ninety- nine years of age, she has seen a few oatmeal cookies. These, she claims, are the best.

Chocolate Chip Oatmeal Cookies

1½ cups flour
1¼ teaspoons baking soda
1 teaspoon salt
1 cup shortening
¾ cup brown sugar
¾ cup sugar
2 eggs
1 teaspoon hot water
1½ cups chopped pecans
1 12-ounce package semisweet chocolate chips
2 cups quick oats
1 teaspoon vanilla

Sift together flour, soda, and salt. In a separate bowl cream together shortening and sugars. Add eggs, one at a time, beating well after each addition. Stir in hot water and flour mixture. Add remaining ingredients. Mix well. Drop from a teaspoon onto a baking sheet. Bake at 375 degrees for 8 to 10 minutes. Yields 10 dozen.

Vicki Brown
Fort Worth

Oatmeal Cookies

1½ cups shortening
2 cups sugar
4 eggs
1 cup milk
4 cups flour
1 teaspoon salt
2 teaspoons cinnamon
1 teaspoon cloves
2 teaspoons baking soda
4 cups quick oats
1 pound raisins
1 cup chopped walnuts

Cream shortening and blend in sugar. Beat in eggs. Stir in milk. Sift together flour, salt, cinnamon, cloves, and soda and blend into shortening mixture. Fold in oats, raisins, and walnuts. Drop in walnut-size mounds on a greased cookie sheet about 2 inches apart. Bake at 375 degrees for 11 to 12 minutes. Makes about 9 dozen.

Laurel M. Anderson
San Antonio

Grandma Noll's Sand Tarts

4 cups flour
½ pound butter or margarine
2 cups sugar
3 eggs
1 egg white
granulated sugar
cinnamon
chopped nuts or nut halves

Cut butter into flour, then add sugar; mix well. Add eggs, mix well, and refrigerate overnight. Roll out dough as thin as possible and cut into 2-inch rounds. Brush tops with egg white and sprinkle with granulated sugar and cinnamon. Place chopped nuts or nut halves on top. Bake at 350 degrees for about 10 to 12 minutes.

Ira G. Gasser
Garland

My dad's roots are in the Pennsylvania Dutch country of Lancaster County, Pennsylvania. Every Christmas my grandparents sent us our Christmas presents in a large box, along with a large tin of these sand tarts. To this day, there are no other sand tarts in the world like these.

Washday Cookies

½ cup shortening
½ cup butter
2 cups brown sugar
2 eggs, well beaten
¼ cup hot water
1 teaspoon baking soda
1 cup flaked coconut
1 teaspoon vanilla
4½ cups flour
¼ teaspoon salt
1½ teaspoons baking powder
pecan halves

Cream together shortening, butter, and brown sugar; add eggs. Dissolve soda in hot water and add to shortening mixture. Stir, then add coconut and vanilla. Sift flour, salt, and baking powder together. Add to shortening mixture and mix well. Refrigerate. Shape dough into small balls and flatten with fork to make a washboard design. Top with pecan halves and bake at 375 degrees for 8 to 10 minutes. Makes about 5 dozen.

Dorothy E. Scherlen
Borger

In the old days, the housewife would get up extra early and mix up this dough for cookies, then put it in the icebox to chill while doing the weekly washing. In the evening, when the wood stove was hot from cooking supper, she would bake the cookies. This has been my favorite recipe for well over fifty years.

Surprise Brownies

1 package German chocolate cake mix
1 cup chopped nuts
1 stick butter, melted
½ cup evaporated milk
1 package milk chocolate chips
50 caramels
⅓ cup evaporated milk

Mix together cake mix, nuts, butter, and ½ cup evaporated milk. Press half of the mixture into a greased 9″ × 13″ pan. Bake at 350 degrees for 4 minutes. Remove from oven and sprinkle chocolate chips on top. Melt caramels in ⅓ cup evaporated milk and drizzle over chips. Sprinkle with remaining half of cake mixture and bake an additional 12 minutes. Cut while warm.

Ohleen Leatherwood
Timpson

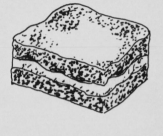

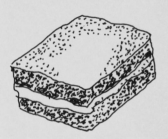

Walnut–Cream Cheese Brownies

4 1-ounce squares unsweetened chocolate
¾ cup butter, softened
4 eggs
½ teaspoon salt
2 teaspoons vanilla, divided
2½ cups sugar, divided
1 cup flour
1 cup chopped walnuts or pecans
1 8-ounce package cream cheese

Melt chocolate in the top of a double boiler over hot water; set aside to cool. Cream butter; gradually add 2 cups sugar, beating well. Add 3 eggs, one at a time, beating well after each addition. Stir in melted chocolate. Add flour, salt, walnuts, and 1 teaspoon vanilla, stirring well. Pour batter into a greased and floured 9″ × 13″ pan. Beat cream cheese until smooth; gradually add remaining ½ cup sugar, beating well. Add remaining egg and 1 teaspoon vanilla, beating well. Drop by heaping tablespoons over chocolate mixture, swirling into mixture with a knife. Bake at 350 degrees for 45 minutes. Cool and cut into squares.

Janice Davis
Richardson

Peanut Butter Bars

1 cup butter or margarine
1 cup white sugar
1 cup brown sugar
2 eggs
2 teaspoons vanilla
½ cup plus 3 tablespoons peanut butter
2 cups flour
½ teaspoon salt
1 teaspoon baking soda
2 cups quick oats

CHOCOLATE FROSTING
⅓ cup butter
1 cup powdered sugar
1½ tablespoons cocoa
½ teaspoon vanilla

Combine butter and sugars; add eggs, vanilla, and peanut butter; mix well. Add remaining ingredients and spread evenly in a greased 9″ × 13″ pan. Bake at 350 degrees for 20 to 25 minutes. Do not overbake. Cool. To make frosting, beat all ingredients together well and spread on cooled peanut butter mixture. Cut into bars.

Lois Coleman
Normangee

Old-Timey Tea Cakes

1 cup shortening
2½ cups sugar
3 eggs
1 tablespoon vanilla
4 teaspoons baking powder
5 cups flour

Cream together shortening, sugar, eggs, vanilla, and baking powder. Add half the flour and mix well. Add remaining flour, using hands to mix. Divide dough into three portions; on a floured board roll out each portion ¼ inch thick. Cut out with a cookie cutter. Place on greased cookie sheets. Bake at 400 degrees for 8 to 10 minutes or until cookies are brown on the bottom but not on top.

Sandra Mooney
Edgewood

These are the kind of cookies Grandma made when there wasn't much sugar available.

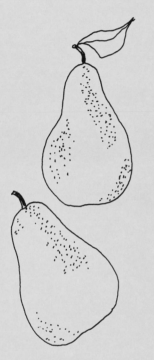

Sallie's Pear Squares

1½ cups sugar
1½ cups cooked and mashed pears
4 eggs
¾ cup vegetable oil
2 cups flour
2 teaspoons baking soda
½ teaspoon cinnamon
½ teaspoon ginger
½ teaspoon nutmeg
½ teaspoon salt
1 teaspoon vanilla
¾ cup chopped pecans (optional)
1½ cups sifted powdered sugar
3 tablespoons butter, melted
⅔ cup milk

Cream together sugar, pears, eggs, and oil. Sift together flour, soda, spices, and salt and add to creamed mixture. Add vanilla and pecans. Spread on a greased and floured 12″ × 18″ × 1″ cookie sheet and bake at 350 degrees for 25 minutes or until toothpick inserted in center comes out clean. Mix together powdered sugar, butter, and milk and spread on warm cake. Cut into 3-inch squares.

Sallie Smith
Anderson

CANDIES

Cinnamon Pecans

1 egg white
1 teaspoon water
2 cups pecan halves
½ cup sugar
½ teaspoon cinnamon
½ teaspoon salt

Beat egg white with water until frothy. Mix pecan halves into egg white mixture. Mix sugar, cinnamon, and salt together and sprinkle over pecans. Spread on a cookie sheet lined with foil and bake at 200 degrees for 1 hour. Stir every 15 minutes.

Doreene Allen
Abilene

Candied Peanuts

3 cups raw peanuts
1 cup sugar
½ cup water
salt to taste

Mix all ingredients in a saucepan over medium-low heat. Stirring constantly, cook until dry. Pour onto a greased cookie sheet. Bake at 300 degrees for 10 minutes. Stir, sprinkle with salt, and spread out over pan. Cook for 15 more minutes. Stir and cook 10 minutes more.

Laura Bailey
Brownsboro

Buckeye Balls

1 stick margarine
1 pound powdered sugar
1½ cups peanut butter
1 teaspoon vanilla
1 12-ounce package chocolate chips
½ bar paraffin

Combine margarine, powdered sugar, peanut butter, and vanilla. Mix well and form into 1-inch balls; chill. Melt chocolate and paraffin in a double boiler. Insert toothpicks into chilled balls and dip into hot chocolate, leaving small area at top uncoated to resemble buckeyes.

Ann Sanders
Rowlett

Coconut Date Balls

1 stick margarine
¾ cup sugar
1 cup chopped dates
2 eggs, beaten well
1 cup broken pecans
1 cup Rice Krispies
1 teaspoon vanilla
1½ cups shredded coconut

In a large skillet over low heat, heat butter to melting, then stir in sugar, dates, and eggs. Stirring constantly, continue cooking slowly until mixture thickens. Remove from heat and stir in pecans, Rice Krispies, and vanilla. Cool. Sprinkle coconut onto waxed paper. Form dough into balls (about 1 teaspoon each) and roll balls in coconut. Store in airtight container.

Mayon Gibson
Rowlett

Haystacks

2 cups Cap'n Crunch cereal
2 cups Rice Krispies
2 cups cocktail peanuts or walnuts
2 cups small pretzels
1 package Almond Bark candy

In a large bowl combine cereals, nuts, and pretzels. Melt Almond Bark in microwave, stirring occasionally. Pour over cereal mixture and mix well. Drop by spoonfuls onto waxed paper.

Elsie Mae Lohner
Gainesville

Peanut Butter–Honey Pecan Balls

1 cup peanut butter
1 cup dry milk
1 cup honey
¼ cup toasted wheat bran
¼ cup wheat germ
½ teaspoon vanilla
chopped pecans

Mix together all ingredients except pecans. Shape into small balls. Roll in chopped pecans. Serve in individual paper candy cups.

Sister Mary Beth, IWBS
Yoakum

Pecan Puffs

2 packages caramels
1 tablespoon butter or margarine
1 large package marshmallows
8 cups fine-chopped pecans

In the top of a double boiler, melt caramels with butter, stirring several times. Spear marshmallow with fork and hold over melted caramel. Using another fork or knife, coat marshmallow with caramel, then dip into pecans and pat gently so that pecans will stick. Push puff off fork onto waxed paper to cool. Repeat until all marshmallows are dipped. (Caramel may have to be reheated if it gets too stiff.) Wrap each puff separately in plastic wrap. Store in tight container.

Mrs. John Watts
Palestine

Microwave Pralines

2 cups firmly packed light brown sugar
¾ cup half-and-half
3 tablespoons butter or margarine
1½ cups chopped pecans
⅛ teaspoon cinnamon
⅛ teaspoon salt

Combine sugar, half-and-half, and butter in a large glass mixing bowl. Microwave on high power for 12 to 14 minutes, or until a small quantity dropped into cold water forms a soft ball (235 degrees). Add chopped pecans, cinnamon, and salt. Cool until lukewarm. Beat until creamy smooth. Drop by teaspoonfuls onto lightly greased waxed paper.

Buena Boron
Dallas

Pecan Pralines

2 cups sugar
1 teaspoon baking soda
1 cup buttermilk
⅛ teaspoon salt
2 tablespoons butter
2½ cups pecan halves

In a large, heavy saucepan combine sugar, soda, buttermilk, and salt. Cook over high heat for 5 minutes (or to 210 degrees on candy thermometer), stirring frequently and scraping bottom of pan. Add butter and pecans. Continue cooking, stirring constantly and scraping bottom and sides of pan, for about 5 minutes or until candy reaches soft-ball stage (234 degrees). Remove from heat and cool slightly. Beat until thick and creamy. Drop from a tablespoon onto waxed paper. Cool. Makes about 18 2-inch pralines.

Leila Doris Kelley
Valentine

Microwave Peanut Brittle

1 cup sugar
1 cup raw peanuts
½ cup light corn syrup
1 tablespoon margarine
1 teaspoon vanilla
1 teaspoon baking soda

Combine sugar, peanuts, and syrup in a 2-quart microwave-safe bowl. Cook on high power for 8 minutes. Stir in margarine and vanilla and microwave for 1 additional minute. Add baking soda and stir, then pour quickly onto a greased cookie sheet. Spread in a very thin layer. Let cool completely, then break into pieces and store in an airtight container. (Do not attempt to make this candy when the weather is damp as it will be sticky.)

Wylene Taft
Garland

Surprise Sweet Potato Candy

2 cups sugar
½ cup margarine
1 cup evaporated milk
½ cup raw grated sweet potatoes
2 cups small marshmallows
1 cup graham cracker crumbs
2 teaspoons vanilla
2 cups chopped pecans

In a large saucepan combine sugar, margarine, and milk and cook over medium heat, stirring frequently, until mixture boils. Add sweet potatoes. While stirring, continue to boil until mixture reaches soft-ball stage (235 degrees on a candy thermometer). Remove from heat and add marshmallows and graham cracker crumbs. Stir until marshmallows are melted and well blended. Add vanilla and pecans, mixing well. Pour into a buttered 9-inch square baking dish. Cool completely before cutting into squares.

Joyco O. Foss
Amarillo

This is an old German recipe.

This recipe was a prizewinner at the Texas State Fair in 1961 and at the Oklahoma State Fair in 1967.

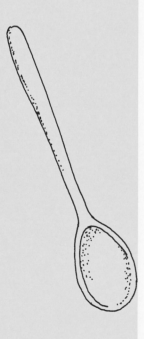

Date Loaf Candy

2 cups sugar
1 cup milk
1 package dates, chopped
1 tablespoon butter
2 cups chopped pecans

Mix all ingredients except pecans and boil over medium heat until mixture reaches soft-ball stage. Beat until stiff; add pecans. Pour out on damp cloth, roll up, and chill. Slice.

Mildred Ritchie
Lubbock

Date-Nut Confection

2½ cups pitted chopped dates
2 cups sugar
1 cup milk
2 cups chopped pecans
1 teaspoon almond extract
1 pound powdered sugar

Combine dates, sugar, and milk in a saucepan. Cook over medium heat, stirring until sugar is dissolved. Cook to soft-ball stage (236 degrees). Remove from heat. Add almond extract and pecans, mixing well. Add about half of the powdered sugar and mix. Spread remaining powdered sugar on waxed paper. Turn mixture out onto powdered sugar and knead, mixing well. Form a roll about 1½ inches in diameter. Cool and cut into ¼-inch slices.

Roaul L. Begley
Arlington

Million-Dollar Candy

3 Hershey chocolate bars
3 6-ounce packages chocolate chips
1 jar marshmallow cream
4 cups sugar
1 large can evaporated milk
1 teaspoon vanilla
½ stick butter
1 pound chopped pecans

In a large bowl break Hershey bars into pieces; add chocolate chips and marshmallow cream. In a 4½-quart saucepan, mix sugar and milk. Bring to a rolling boil and cook for 4½ minutes, stirring constantly. Remove from heat and add chocolate mixture. Stir until chocolate is melted. Add vanilla, butter, and pecans. When butter is melted, pour into a buttered 9″ × 13″ pan. Cool and cut into squares. Makes 5 pounds.

John and Cindy Wright
Crandall

Leche Quemada

2 cups pecans (small or broken pieces)
½ cup margarine
⅔ cup firmly packed brown sugar
1 14-ounce can sweetened condensed milk
1 teaspoon vanilla

Place pecans on a large glass plate and microwave on high power for 8 minutes, stirring at 2-minute intervals. Set aside. In an 8-cup microwave-safe bowl, microwave margarine on high power for 1 minute. Stir in brown sugar and milk until blended. Microwave on high power for 7 minutes, stirring at 2-minute intervals. Beat with a wooden spoon about 5 minutes or until stiff. Stir in vanilla and reserved pecans. Spread in a lightly greased 8-inch square glass dish. Chill until firm. Cut into squares. Makes 1½ pounds.

Mildred R. Kneupper
New Braunfels

Coffee Cream Fudge

2 cups brown sugar
¼ cup heavy cream
½ cup strong coffee
⅛ teaspoon salt
2 tablespoons butter
1 cup chopped nuts

In a saucepan combine all ingredients except nuts and cook until mixture reaches soft-ball stage, then cool to room temperature. Beat until thick and creamy, add nuts, and pour into a buttered pan. Cool.

Luella Vanderveer
Bandera

Sour Cream Fudge

2 cups sugar
1 cup sour cream
½ cup light corn syrup
1 teaspoon vanilla
1 cup chopped nuts

In a saucepan mix sugar, sour cream, and syrup and cook until mixture reaches soft-ball stage. Add vanilla and nuts and beat until creamy and thick. Pour into a buttered 8″ × 8″ dish and chill.

Shirley Embrey
San Antonio

My GranGran taught me how to make this. I've been making it since I was seven. Now I'm nine. We make it every summer. My GranGran found an old Texas cookbook in her attic, and I decided to make this.

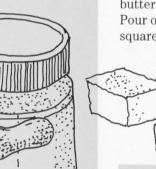

Texas Peanut Butter Fudge

2 cups sugar
2 tablespoons light corn syrup
⅛ teaspoon salt
¾ cup canned milk
1 teaspoon vanilla
⅓ cup peanut butter

In a deep saucepan, mix together sugar, syrup, salt, and milk. Cook over medium heat until mixture reaches soft-ball stage (234 degrees on a candy thermometer). Cool and add peanut butter. Beat vigorously until mixture shines and starts to thicken. Pour out onto a buttered platter or square pan. Cool and cut into squares.

Allison Lashlee
Highlands

Save-Your-Sugar French Fudge

3 6-ounce packages semisweet chocolate chips
1 can Eagle Brand sweetened condensed milk
1½ teaspoons vanilla
pinch of salt
½ cups chopped nuts

In the top of a double boiler, melt chocolate chips over hot water. Remove from heat, add sweetened condensed milk, vanilla, salt, and nuts. Stir until smooth. Turn into a waxed-paper-lined 8-inch square pan. Chill. Store in airtight container.

Louise Sharp
Big Spring

Creamy Chocolate Fudge

2 cups sugar
3 tablespoons cocoa
pinch of salt
⅓ cup light corn syrup
1 cup whipping cream
1 teaspoon vanilla
3 tablespoons butter
1 cup chopped pecans

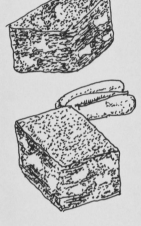

Combine sugar, cocoa, and salt, blending well. Add syrup and cream. Cook over medium heat, stirring, and bring to a boil. Do not stir after boiling point is reached. Reduce heat and cook until mixture reaches soft-ball stage. Cool. Add vanilla and butter. Beat well. Add nuts. Spoon by teaspoonfuls onto waxed paper. Makes 30 pieces.

Clair Bradford
Flower Mound

Mama's Divinity

2½ cups sugar
½ cup water
½ cup light corn syrup
¼ teaspoon salt
2 egg whites, beaten stiff
1 cup pecans
1 teaspoon vanilla or other flavoring

Boil sugar, water, syrup, and salt until mixture forms a firm ball in cold water or makes a thread when dripped from a spoon. Pour into egg whites and beat until mixture begins to thicken. Add nuts and vanilla and beat well. Pour into a well-greased pan or platter. Cool and cut into squares.

Ira Ray
Brownwood

This recipe dates back to 1896.

Ira Ray is a motorcycle enthusiast and a member of the Hadacol Angels, a motocycle club for senior citizens. Some members of the club have been riding together for nearly half a century.

Patience

1 cup canned milk
3 cups sugar, divided
2 tablespoons butter or margarine
2 cups chopped pecans
1 teaspoon vanilla

In a saucepan mix milk and 2 cups sugar and bring to a boil. Meanwhile, in another saucepan melt remaining 1 cup sugar over low heat, stirring constantly. When melted sugar is brown, pour into boiling milk and sugar. Cook until mixture forms a firm ball in cold water. Add butter and pecans, remove from heat, and beat well; add vanilla. Transfer to a buttered dish. Cool and cut into squares.

Peggy Jean Heil
Gonzales

PRESERVES & RELISHES

Mock Apricot Preserves

6 cups peeled and shredded zucchini squash
6 cups sugar
½ cup lemon juice
1 large can crushed pineapple
1 package Sure-Jell
1 large or 2 small packages apricot Jell-O

In a saucepan mix all ingredients except Sure-Jell and Jell-O and cook 25 minutes. Add Sure-Jell and cook 5 minutes more. Remove from heat, add Jell-O, and stir until cool. Put in jars, seal, and refrigerate overnight.

Mrs. Russell L. Elkins
Lometa

This recipe won first place at the 1989 State Fair of Texas.

Blackberry Preserves

5 pounds whole blackberries, washed
6 cups sugar
¼ cup lemon juice

In a kettle heat berries over low heat; when juice begins to boil, add sugar and lemon juice. Boil over high heat about 20 minutes or until syrup thickens. Place in hot sterilized jars, seal, and process in a hot water bath for 10 minutes. Makes about 8 cups.

Ira G. Gasser
Garland

Strawberry-Fig Preserves

3 cups mashed figs (about 20 medium figs)
1 6-ounce package strawberry Jell-O
3 cups sugar
2 tablespoons lemon juice

In a heavy saucepan mix figs, Jell-O, sugar, and lemon juice and bring to a boil over medium heat. Continue boiling for 3 minutes, stirring frequently. Pour quickly into hot, sterilized jars, wipe tops, and run knife blade around edges to release any air bubbles. Seal at once. Cool, then store in refrigerator. Makes 5 cups. Can be frozen for entended storage.

Kathy Jo Gamelin
Houston

Fig Preserves

8 cups figs
8 cups sugar
3 cups water
4 lemon slices or 1 tablespoon lemon juice

Wash, dry gently, and halve each fig. Pack in measuring cup but do not mash. Place in large kettle. Combine with sugar and lemon slices. Cook over low heat until fruit is clear and transparent. Fill sterilized jars and seal. Makes 4 or 5 pints.

Pepper Crisp
Midlothian

This won the blue ribbon at the 1981 State Fair of Texas.

Cantaloupe Preserves

4 or 5 medium ripe cantaloupes, ground
2 20-ounce cans crushed pineapple
5 pounds sugar
1½ teaspoons cloves

In a heavy stainless steel pot, bring all ingredients to a boil, then reduce heat and boil for 2 to 3 hours or until thickened. Stir frequently to prevent sticking. Pack in clean hot jars and seal. Makes about 12 pints.

Stanley Golla
Adkins

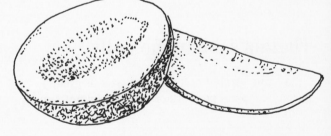

This recipe is believed to have originated in Germany; it was handed down through the generations in the late 1800s. It's best when served on hot buttered biscuits.

Bessie's Spicy Watermelon Preserves

4 pounds watermelon rind
½ cup salt in 1 gallon water
8 cups sugar
8 cups water
4 lemons, sliced
4 teaspoons cloves
4 teaspoons stick cinnamon
red or green food coloring (optional)

This recipe was passed down from my great-grandmother, who was a Cherokee medicine woman.

Soak rinds in salt water overnight. Remove and cook in fresh water for 30 minutes. Drain. Make a syrup of water and sugar; add sliced lemons. Tie spices in cheesecloth bag and boil in syrup for 5 minutes. Add rinds and cook until transparent and clear. Add food coloring. Remove spice bag and ladle rinds into sterilized jars and seal.

Dianne Wilson
San Angelo

Rose Petal Jelly

1 cup rose petals (from roses grown without pesticides)
¾ cup water
2½ cups sugar
juice of 1 lemon
1 package Sure-Jell
¾ cup water

Trim white from ends of petals. Combine rose petals and water and blend until smooth, then gradually add sugar. Blend until dissolved. Add lemon juice. In a saucepan mix Sure-Jell and water. Boil over high heat for 1 minute, then add to rose petal mixture. Cool until thick, pour into jars, and refrigerate (or freeze in plastic containers).

Nan Butcher
Grapeland

Thelma's Jalapeño Jelly

2 cups fine-ground bell peppers (red or green)
4 small jalapeño peppers or 6 small red hot peppers
5 cups sugar
1½ cups white vinegar
2 6-ounce packages Certo

Remove seeds and stems from peppers and grind with finest blade of food grinder; drain well (press with rubber spatula if needed). In a large saucepan, mix ground peppers, sugar, and vinegar. Bring to full boil and boil for 1 minute, then stir in Certo. Bring to boil again and boil for 30 seconds. Remove from heat and let stand 10 minutes. Skim and pour into hot sterilized jars. Makes 8 to 9 half-pints. Especially good served with roast beef or as an appetizer spread over cream cheese.

Rosemary Pinson
Dallas

Prickly Pear Cactus Jelly

prickly pears
juice of 1 lemon
1 package Sure-Jell
3 cups sugar

Using metal tongs to handle prickly pears, rinse in water, cut in half, and place in a large pot. Cover with water and bring to a boil; boil until tender, mashing with a potato masher while cooking. Strain juice through a cotton bag to make 3 cups liquid. (Cactus juice can be frozen at this point for later use.) Mix cactus juice and Sure-Jell. Bring to a boil, stirring, then add sugar and follow directions on Sure-Jell package regarding cooking time. Add lemon juice. Spoon off any film and pour into sterile jars. Seal with melted paraffin and cool. Screw lids on jars securely.

Winifred Thompson
Three Rivers

Pumpkin Butter Jam

10 cups peeled pumpkin, ground
juice of 2 lemons
1 tablespoon ginger
1 tablespoon cinnamon
½ teaspoon allspice
¾ teaspoon salt
1¼ cups brown sugar
1 cup Karo syrup

Combine pumpkin, lemon juice, spices, salt, sugar, and syrup. Let stand overnight. Then add water and boil gently until pumpkin is clear and mixture is thick. Pour into sterilized jars and seal while hot. Parboil 5 minutes.

Sue Enos Layton
Fort Worth

This won me Best of Show in 1984 in a special category of jams and jellies made with Karo syrup.

Ripe Tomato Relish

1 gallon ripe tomatoes
4 large onions
2 cups vinegar
1½ cups sugar
2 teaspoons black pepper
1 teaspoon nutmeg
1 teaspoon allspice
2 hot green peppers (optional)
2 teaspoons salt
1 teaspoon cinnamon
1 teaspoon dry mustard

In large heavy pot combine all ingredients and cook until some of the liquid is evaporated. Seal in jars while hot.

Hazel Davis
Comanche

Mary's Quick Corn Relish

1 16-ounce can whole-kernel corn
1 tablespoon cornstarch
2 tablespoons onion flakes
2 teaspoons celery seed
⅓ cup sugar
⅓ cup vinegar
⅓ cup sweet pickle relish
1 4-ounce jar pimientos, drained and diced

Drain corn and set aside, reserving ¼ cup of the liquid. In a saucepan, blend liquid with cornstarch. Add drained corn and remaining ingredients. Simmer 10 minutes, stirring occasionally. Serve hot or cold with meat, fish, or poultry. Makes about 2½ cups.

Nan Fassig
Plano

Hot Jalapeño Relish

1 pound jalapeño peppers, chopped
4 bell peppers, chopped
2 large onions, chopped
1 cup oil
1 large tomato, sliced
1 20-ounce bottle catsup
1 15-ounce can tomatoes
1 cup beer
2 tablespoons garlic
¼ cup Worcestershire sauce
salt and pepper to taste

In a large kettle, combine all ingredients and bring to a boil.
Reduce heat and simmer 2 hours. Seal in sterilized jars. Makes
1 gallon.

Lewis Meinzer
Childress

Lillie's Chow Chow

1 gallon tomatoes
1 cup water
5 sweet peppers
4 or 5 hot peppers
several onions
1 stalk celery
1 large head cabbage
½ cup salt
3 cups vinegar or more to taste
2 cups sugar
2 teaspoons cinnamon
2 teaspoons allspice
2 teaspoons tumeric
2 teaspoons dry mustard
juice of 4 lemons

In a large kettle, combine all ingredients except lemon juice.
Bring to a boil and then cook at least 1 hour. Add more water and
vinegar if needed. Add lemon juice near end of cooking time.
Pour into sterilized jars and seal. Makes 8 pints.

Joyce N. Kennedy
San Antonio

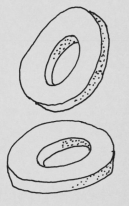

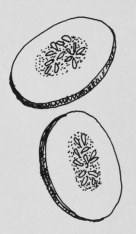

Apple Ring Pickles

10 to 12 very large cucumbers
2 cups pickling lime
water
4 cups white vinegar, divided
1 tablespoon alum
1 ounce red food coloring
5 pounds sugar
12 sticks cinnamon
20 ounces cinnamon candies
3 cups water

Peel, slice, and core cucumbers. Slice into rings ¼ inch thick. Dissolve lime in enough water to cover cucumbers and soak for 24 hours. Drain and rinse cucumber slices in fresh water several times to remove all traces of lime. Then soak for 3 hours in fresh water and drain. Combine 1 cup white vinegar, alum, food coloring, and water to cover cucumber slices. Add cucumber slices and simmer for 3 hours; drain and discard solution. Mix remaining ingredients and bring to a boil. When candies are completely dissolved, remove from heat and add cucumber slices and enough water to completely cover. Let stand for 24 hours. Remove cucumber slices and bring syrup to a boil again; pour over slices. Repeat this step for three more days. On the fourth day, place pickles into sterilized jars, cover with syrup, and seal.

Sophie Neumann
Marlin

Frozen Cucumber Pickles

5 cups thin-sliced cucumbers
1 cup thin-sliced onions
2 tablespoons salt
1½ cups sugar
1 cup vinegar
½ teaspoon mustard seed
½ teaspoon celery seed

In a glass or enamel bowl or a crock, mix cucumbers, onions, and salt. Refrigerate for 2 hours. Combine remaining ingredients and bring to a boil; remove from heat and cool. Drain cucumbers, pour syrup over cucumbers, place in freezer containers, and freeze.

Mary Martin
Hunt

Pickled Banana Peppers

sweet or hot banana peppers
2 cups vinegar
1 cup water
1 cup sugar

Quarter peppers and remove stems and seeds. Pack tightly in pint jars. Combine vinegar, water, and sugar and bring to a boil. Boil 2 minutes; pour over peppers. Cap with hot lids and seal. Makes about 3 pints. These peppers are extra crisp.

Marticia Wallace
Denison

Pickled Okra

2 pounds small fresh okra
5 cloves garlic
5 small hot peppers
1 quart white vinegar
½ cup water
8 tablespoons salt
1 tablespoon celery seeds (optional)
1 tablespoon mustard seeds (optional)

Wash okra and pack in five sterilized pint jars. Place 1 clove of garlic and 1 hot pepper in each jar. Mix vinegar, water, salt, celery seeds, and mustard seeds and bring to a boil. Pour boiling mixture into each jar and seal. Let stand 3 weeks before using.

Louise Phillips
Amarillo

Pear Mincemeat

½ bushel pears, pared and cored
2 pounds raisins
2 sticks margarine
1½ cups vinegar
2 teaspoons cinnamon
2 teaspoon allspice
2 teaspoons cloves
3½ cups sugar

Chop or grind pears and raisins. Place in a large kettle and add margarine and vinegar. Tie spices in a cheesecloth bag and drop into kettle. Add sugar and mix well. Cook over slow heat for 1 hour and 20 minutes. Seal in jars. Boil in hot water bath for 15 minutes.

Dorothy Harris
Azle

Pickled Green Tomatoes

3 quarts white vinegar
6 cups sugar
1 cup salt
2 tablespoons black pepper
2 gallons thin-sliced small green tomatoes
½ gallon thin-sliced onions
1 quart sliced hot green peppers
powdered alum

Heat vinegar to boiling and add sugar, salt, and pepper. Pack tomatoes, onions, and hot peppers into jars and cover with boiling liquid. Add a pinch of alum to each jar. Wipe the rims of the jars and seal tightly. Cool away from drafts and then store at least three weeks before serving.

Greg Haston
Angleton

This was a blue-ribbon winner at the 1988 State Fair of Texas.

Mother's Chili Sauce

2 quarts fresh tomatoes
1 quart onions
3 hot peppers (or more to taste)
1 bell pepper
1 cup sugar
2 cups apple cider vinegar
2 tablespoons salt
1 tablespoon cinnamon

Chop tomatoes, onions, hot peppers, and bell pepper. Add remaining ingredients and cook in a large pot over medium heat for 2 hours or until thickened, Pour into sterilized pint jars and seal. Place in hot water bath for 7 minutes. Makes 4 to 5 pints.

LaNelle Toney
Kaufman

Old-Fashioned Bread and Butter Pickles

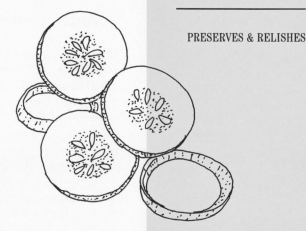

4 quarts unpeeled cucumbers, sliced thin
6 medium white onions, sliced
1 bell pepper
3 cloves garlic, minced
⅓ cup canning salt
5 cups sugar
3 cups apple cider vinegar
2 tablespoons mustard seeds
1½ teaspoons celery seeds
1½ teaspoons tumeric

Combine cucumbers, onions, bell pepper, garlic, and salt. Cover with cracked ice and mix thoroughly. Let stand 3 hours. Drain well. Add remaining ingredients to cucumber mixture and bring to a boil. Pour into hot sterilized jars (pickles should be packed snug but not crushed). Run knife blade around sides of jars to release air bubbles. Wipe mouth of jar with clean, wet cloth. Slightly tighten lid and set aside to cool. When cool, completely tighten lids and store.

Doris and Carl Riedel
Mesquite

Carl Riedel is the manager of Samuell Farm. The 640-acre farm, owned by the City of Dallas, teaches visitors about farm life.

Squash Pickles

10 cups sliced yellow squash
1 bell pepper, sliced
4 large onions, sliced
5 hot peppers, sliced
4 tablespoons salt
4½ cups sugar
2½ tablespoons tumeric
1 teaspoon black pepper
2½ cups vinegar
½ teaspoon nutmeg
1½ teaspoons celery seeds

Combine squash, bell pepper, onions, and hot peppers. Sprinkle with salt and let stand 10 minutes. Rinse well with water. Add remaining ingredients and transfer to a large kettle. Bring to a boil and cook for 20 minutes. Seal in hot jars. Makes 5 to 6 pints.

Frances Sanders
Garland

Picante Sauce

3 quarts peeled ripe tomatoes
2 cups whole mild jalapeño peppers with caps removed
1 clove garlic, peeled (or 1 tablespoon garlic powder)
2 cups sweet onions
3 tablespoons canning salt
1 tablespoon ground cumin
½ cup sugar
2 cups red wine vinegar

In a food processor chop tomatoes, peppers, and garlic clove. Cut onions into chunks. Combine all ingredients in a large heavy saucepan and mix well. Bring to a boil, stirring frequently and scooping off foam from top. Reduce heat and simmer, stirring frequently, for 45 minutes to 1 hour or until mixture is the desired thickness. Remove from heat, cool, and pour into hot sterilized jars and seal. Place jars in boiling water bath and process 35 minutes. Makes approximately 4 pints.

Hazel Laza
Ennis

BEVERAGES

Alice's Punch

6 cups water
5 cups sugar
1 box cherry or apricot Jell-O
1 large can pineapple juice
2 small cans frozen lemonade
1 teaspoon almond extract

Mix all ingredients well. Then add water equal to the quantity of the total ingredients. Freeze, stirring every hour until mixture becomes a slush.

Diana Schmittou
Aubrey

Banana Punch

3 cups sugar
6 cups water
6 large bananas, pureed
1 48-ounce can pineapple juice
1 12-ounce can frozen orange juice
juice of 2 lemons
3 quarts ginger ale

Combine all ingredients except ginger ale and freeze. When ready to serve, let thaw until slushy. Add ginger ale and mix well. Makes 15 to 20 servings.

Nina Fair
Covington

This was served at our golden wedding anniversary party.

Golden Punch

½ gallon vanilla ice cream
1 large can crushed pineapple
4 large bananas
1 jar maraschino cherries
3 large bottles 7-Up or ginger ale
yellow ice cubes

Cut ice cream into three pieces and place in punch bowl. Add fruit, 7-Up, and ice cubes. (To make yellow ice cubes, add yellow food coloring to water in ice tray.)

Frances Willoughby
Amarillo

Banana Fruit Punch

2 3-ounce packages strawberry Jell-O
1 cup sugar
2 cups boiling water
6 cups cold water
1½ cups concentrated lemon juice
2 cups pineapple juice
5 cups orange juice
5 bananas, mashed
1 quart ginger ale
1 pint whole strawberries
3 bananas, sliced

Dissolve Jell-O and sugar in boiling water; stir until dissolved. Add cold water, lemon juice, and pineapple and orange juices. Chill. Just before serving, mash bananas until creamy, stir into punch, and add ginger ale. Garnish with sliced bananas and strawberries. Makes 35 5-ounce servings.

Katherine Crick
Garland

Friendship Tea

1 18-ounce package orange-flavored instant breakfast drink
1 cup sugar
½ cup sweetened lemonade mix
½ cup instant tea
1 3-ounce package apricot Jell-O
2½ teaspoons cinnamon
1 teaspoon cloves

Combine all ingredients in a large bowl, stirring well. Store mix in an airtight container. To use, add 1½ teaspoons mix to 1 cup boiling water. Stir well. Makes about 50 servings.

Trish Davis
Lubbock

Almond Tea

1½ cups sugar
2 tablespoons lemon juice
2 quarts water
2 cups strong tea
1 teaspoon almond extract
1 teaspoon vanilla extract
6 tablespoons lemon juice

Boil sugar, lemon juice, and water, then add remaining ingredients. Serve hot.

Valerie Addington
Lubbock

This was used by many in the era between 1929 and 1934. Cream can also be added to improve the taste.

Depression Coffee

2 cups wheat bran
1 pint yellow cornmeal
3 eggs, well beaten
1 cup molasses

Mix wheat bran and cornmeal. Add eggs and molasses, then beat well. Spread in a shallow pan and bake at 250 degrees until dry, stirring often to prevent burning or scorching. Two handfuls serves four people.

Helen Luckenbach Nelson
Kerrville

Hot Chocolate Mix

1 large container Nestle's drink mix
1 medium box Carnation dry milk
1 large jar Cremora
1 2-pound package powdered sugar

Mix all ingredients and store in an airtight container. To use, mix 3 to 4 heaping teaspoons to 1 cup boiling water. Marshmallows can be added on top.

Carla Richardson
Temple

INDEX